A Graveyard Called Two Bits

How to Succeed at War without Really ~~Trying~~ *Dying*

A Memoir
by
Brad L. Smith

Dedicated to Donna, my long-suffering wife; and to Christine, my slightly less suffering daughter . . . but only slightly. Thanks for always being there for me.

Table of Contents

Foreword: Two Bits

The comatose cemetery overlooked the valley of ripening rice. Undisturbed, its stepped pyramids of earth—round, not rectangular, and markerless—spoke of a different take on life and death. This was Bong Son, Binh Dinh Province, South Vietnam. The year was 1966.

Men with minds came first. They put fists to chins and observed. They put instruments to eyes and measured. They put pens to paper and recorded. Then they looked at one another, nodded, and left.

Men with machines came next. Heavy equipment scooped up the small mounds—nameless, but not forgotten—and used them to fill in depressions on the peaceful plateau. They covered the clay with steel sheets, and then surrounded it all with coiled Rattlers of barbed wire. Then they left, too.

No doors made for an unobstructed view, as well as an air-conditioned ride.

Later, men with malice molted from the skies, as if descending from Mount Olympus itself. They rode in green machines that beat the air into submission, forcing the very heavens to lift them over mountains, jungles, and rivers. Between the mounds of memory that remained—unmarked, unremarkable—they staked their tents, living and sleeping between the heaps of death.

Then they dubbed the graveyard-turned-forward-base *Two Bits*—both for what they thought of its worth . . . and what they thought of their chances.

For this Vietnamese cemetery was destined to be the home of the killingest unit of the killingest division of the Vietnam War. This pile of peasant remains was to be the forward base for 770 men responsible for half the kills of the entire 19,500-man 1st Air Cavalry Division—the 1st Squadron/9th Cavalry Regiment; the legendary, the lethal 1/9th Cav!

Finally, I arrived at the age of 19—shy, skinny, but ready to win the war. And like two and a half million other Vietnam veterans—including 58,000 killed and 300,000 wounded—and all their families and friends, I was denied that victory. "War is Hell," said General William Tecumseh Sherman. He was talking about the Civil War, which only half the country lost. In the Vietnam War, for the first time in American history, the whole country lost.

I was one of those sore losers, and that's not how I wanted it. From my earliest recollections, I had been groomed for winning—not losing—at war.

Chapter 1: Playing at War

Until I was ten, I lived and trained for warfare in Whittier, California. Named for a Quaker and abolitionist poet, the town possessed a kind of poetry of its own, or at least it did in the 1950s. A big backyard was our ground-level world, the visible world, surrounded by a five-foot-high redwood-slat fence. During the day, we climbed our trees and ate walnuts. My friends Freddy, David, Alan, and I became deadly with the long bow. At night, my mutt Meatball (named for my favorite food, after mashed potatoes) would jump that fence. Since her legs were short, she had to vault onto the top, land on her belly, and then kick off again to the other side. She taught me that if you want something badly enough— even if you come up short—you can find a way. She did it enough times to drop a litter of puppies before we had her spayed.

Our real world, though, waited where the back fence left off and summer began. On the other side of those red warning boards, a twenty-foot-wide finger of our property held wonders untold for a bare-foot Southern California boy. There was my dad's compost heap that magically changed leaves into mulch, and an incinerator that turned everything else into ash—until new environmental laws turned it into rubble.

My sunflower plant towered over us. The seeds were impossible to reach, and once reached, even harder to open. We ate carrots out of the garden, and picked red, juicy plums right from the tree house—if we could beat the birds and the worms to them first. A slat-sided clubhouse, courtesy of my dad, provided shelter along with the summertime sustenance. White sugar in the form of cookies, brownies, and the like—to offset too much wholesomeness—was special delivered by Mom.

But the very best of all these wonders began where the property dropped off 30 feet to a watery land below; a wild world of adventure: The Creek!

Since no fence beyond the back fence existed—because no laws existed yet to require one—we just slid down the dirt slope with our six-shooters, cowboy hats, and Army caps. We caught frogs, chopped up crawdads with an entrenching tool for my dog to eat, and generally explored all things natural.

And unnatural. We played at war, shooting verbal volleys at each other, "Bang! Bang! You're dead!" only to fight further word battles with our friends the enemy, "I drew first! No, I did!" But eventually—and with a flare—we all took our turn at dying, always to rise and fight again. I even bought a dummy pineapple hand grenade at the corner Army Surplus store, and then spent hours tossing the cast-iron bomb in my backyard.

That was play. In earnest, my personal odyssey began near the end of elementary school. I came across a translation of *Mao Tse-Tung on Guerrilla Warfare*, written in 1937 after Mao spent ten years formulating its lessons against the Nationalist forces of Chiang Kai-shek. As the first systematic analysis of this hit-and-run form of fighting, it became the textbook for Communists from Fidel Castro to Ho Chi Minh. I read it as part of my private course curriculum to know the enemy.

They say, however, that more things are caught than taught. I think that applies even more so for teachers than they may know. While they're struggling to instill the basics of math, science, and such; their students are busy learning lessons of character, courage, and carriage from them.

That was true for me of my 8th grade teacher, Mr. Robert Lynch. Mr. Lynch was a California-transplant from Massachusetts, but that's not why he stood out. He wasn't a large man by any means—at least not on the outside—but he was fit and trim and Kennedy-handsome. When you're 13 years old, skinny, pimpled, big-nosed, and shy, those attributes seem important, even vital.

Then I found out he had been a Marine in World War II, and that clinched it. John Wayne as Sgt. Striker in "The Sands of Iwo Jima" had pointed the way for me to being a real man. Now, my all-time favorite teacher—squared-jawed, confident, and caring—sold me. After high school, I would join the USMC as a career Marine!

Since I had braces on my teeth until I was 19—and the Armed Forces won't consider you until they are off—I had some time on my hands. My parents wanted me to take at least two years of college before I went to war. They didn't particularly care what college I went to or what I studied, so I signed up for Citrus Junior College to keep them happy and paying the bills while I commuted. My folks were also under the impression that they had to pen their permission for me to be able to join the military if I was under 21. They were mistaken.

When my braces came off, I gave everybody a great big new smile, blew off my classes and finals, and signed up.

My uncorrected 20/400 vision was right at the limit for acceptance into the Marine Corps. A woman Marine Major made an executive decision and rejected my application—along with that of a guy who had been caught as a Peeping Tom when he was 13.

You can't really call it discrimination on her part: she treated both the hard of seeing and the too well of seeing the same.

The Marine Recruiter told me the bad news and then the good: "Even though you can't enlist in the Corps, you can still get in as a draftee. The requirements aren't as tough. All you have to do is volunteer for the draft."

That I did . . . on the very same month the Marine Corps stopped drafting!

So, I was in the U.S. Army. Well, if I had to be in the Army, I would be the best they've got: Airborne, Rangers, Green Berets— "All That I Can Be."

Even then my eyes squinted hard and closed those doors for me. "You'll need an alternate MOS (Mode of Schooling)," said the Sergeant on the physical exam board, "like Medics."

Like Medics. I had a friend who was a Navy Corpsman who I admired, so why not? Sure, I hated needles, but I would be giving, not getting; I'd be the sticker, not the stuckee. I changed my status from draftee to enlistee—two years to three years—to guarantee what I wanted, went back for yet another 12-hour physical, my third, and was on my way.

As a recruitment incentive, the Army had sent me a series of posters rolled up in a cardboard tube. They depicted the U.S. soldier down through history. Two photos per poster represented two wars each; four posters, eight wars. Whoever the photographer was, he had both a sense of history and humor. How he ever got his ideas past the Army censors is a mystery.

The Civil War soldier had a dead chicken tied to his belt—a tribute to the art of foraging. The youthful, even naïve World War I "Doughboy" shared his space with a World War II G.I.—dirty, unshaven, with the stub of a cigar sticking out the corner of his mouth. At his feet lay an equally scruffy old yellow dog, the kind that often followed our boys in the European theater.

The posters were commissioned sometime around 1965 and it showed. The soldier for the Korean War (when 36,000 Americans die in three years of fighting, it's a war, not a conflict!) was shorter, with a weak chin; symbolizing our unpreparedness and inadequacy. The Vietnam War soldier next to him, however, said just the opposite. He was tall, blond, and handsome. His jungle fatigues were new and crisp; a sleek space-age M-16 was slung over his shoulder. And he had his hands on his hips, Superman-style.

In the early 1960s, that's how we felt about our military: super men, dropping from the skies and flying away again at will. With a snap of their fingers, fire rained down on their foes from artillery, gunships, and supersonic fighters. There was no doubt in our minds that we would win. No doubt we would prevail over those Communist guerrillas; those pathetic Viet Cong; those sorry little VC.

Chapter 2: Basic Training

Before my senior year of high school, I spent ten days in the Devil Pups program at the Marine base at San Onofre, California. I got a feel for what Boot Camp would be like. We did 3,000 pushups. We were so stiff and sore that we had to help each other on with our denim fatigue jackets; our arms no longer bent the right way! It was a program designed to discourage kids from dropping out of high school to join up. I didn't drop out, but it didn't discourage me. I still wanted to join the Marines. When I couldn't, and was forced into the Army, I imagined its equivalent training would be a picnic. I was wrong.

Basic Training at Fort Ord, California, was a wakeup call, literally . . .

April 20, 1966
Dear Mom, Dad, Jody, and Sharman,
Just a line before lights out to tell you I'm fine. We arrived here at 1:15 am, and proceeded with induction indoctrination until 4:15 am, slept all of 45 minutes, and then we were up at 5:00 am, wide-eyed and incoherent.
Today, Tuesday, we got our fatigue uniforms—long underwear and all.
I'm feeling better now with most of my diarrhea gone.
The prospect of spending three years here depresses me, though. We get a three-day pass in about five weeks, so I'll see what I can do about coming home.
Give my love to all. I'll write again soon when I'm not so tired. As it is, I haven't had any substantial sleep in two days. I'll get plenty tonight though.
Love, Brad

We had drill instructors just like the Marine Corps, Smokey the Bear hats and all. They ran us hard, but without the abject humiliation programmed into the Corps. The goal wasn't to dismantle us cell by cell, and then pour the quivering remains into some one-size-fits-all iron mold. No, the Army was strictly a numbers racket; it dealt in volume. Basic sought to train a lot of us well enough to survive for a time. Combat would select those who were soldiers and those who weren't. It was kind of a Darwinian approach to death and dying; albeit unnatural selection.

We spent the days trying to stay warm in the mornings, not melt in the afternoons, and not freeze at nights. Forty men had died from meningitis at Fort Ord just before I arrived. The Army burnt 40,000 mattresses in an effort to contain it. They also levied restrictions requiring that we slept with the barrack's windows wide open. The quarantine also kept us bottled up, no three-day passes, and only a few trips to the Post Exchange (PX).

April 27

I've just come back from a private interview concerning my Classification Test Scores. Remember, I was eligible for and took qualification tests for Officers Candidate School (OCS) and Foreign Language School. I passed everything the Army threw at me by an adequate margin, even Electronics (remember my trouble with that in Physics?), Mechanics (Motor Pool), and Infantry. I'm now classified Medical Care and Treatment with access to the Paratroopers on completion of my training. Stateside assignment will be California and foreign duty in Vietnam.

I took these photos in a booth at the PX, risking life and limb in harassment from meandering sergeants and corporals. These are our fatigues and newly designed hats. The upper white tape is for platoon, company, battalion, and brigade numbers; in my case, 2-B-4-1. This particular camera takes pale pictures.

We got our shots this morning. The Army might have removed the needles, but not the sting.

Nothing on my broken retainer, yet. I'll write on developments.

Here's $5 for my phone call to Dan; it helped morale.

Your loving son, Brad

I failed to inform the Army of some of my more clerical skills during this time. When one of their forms asked, "Can you type?" I filled in the box marked "No." In truth, I was a very good typist; but I also had a very good friend, Marshall, who spent two years with the Marines typing in an unbearably hot tent in Vietnam, all because he had filled in the wrong box. When they called him up for a third tour of duty, he went AWOL to Canada. Later, President Jimmy Carter

16

bailed out his butt so he could come home. I voted for Carter twice. Reagan was a better president, but Carter was a better person; if anything, too good for the job.

May 1, Sunday

We finally got some leisure time, so I could get out a letter or two.

Cheryl wrote me twice and gave me quite a lift when I needed it. I've just finished writing her back.

Training has become more intensified. Our first day, we learned to field strip and maintain our M-14 rifles. We drill constantly and attend classes on Military Protocol and Courtesy.

The first week is running slowly though. It is supposed to pick up the second week with extensive Physical Training (PT) and the third and fourth weeks will be spent at the rifle range (I'll like that). The fourth and fifth weeks are hand-to-hand combat and running a 350-yard Obstacle Course. We'll be firing live ammo at this course at simulated battle targets and, at times, be fired at ourselves.

Rounding up the seventh week is mostly review and classroom work with the eighth, and final week, reserved solely for graduation exercises. Graduation should be on a Friday, the 24th of June.

My cold has almost run its course and I've gained five pounds, so don't worry. Missing you all.

Love, Brad

May 22

I'm trying to get a few lines off as often as possible.

We've just returned from the Rifle Range after qualifying in zeroing-in our weapons. I qualified with a shot-group accurate up to 250 meters (about 275 yards), so I'll start going to the Target Detection Range on Tuesday. I qualified on five-out-of-eight of the different positions, which was enough. Two of the positions I failed I couldn't get into because of my leg injury, and the third they didn't let us refire. I zeroed-in my rifle with only three shot groups though, while most of the other guys took as many as 20 or more.

Most of my ear and nose infection has cleared up, as has my vision. My leg troubled me, though, and they allowed me to ride to and from the range. I still can't run on it, but it is improving.

My faith in God has helped me quite a bit through the long hours of training, as I know He will when I'm a Medic and must say to the wounded and maimed, "Coward, take my coward's hand."

Seeing you Sunday stirred the pains of homesickness again, but was good for morale. I love you all very much. God bless and keep you all.

Love, Brad

Chapter 3: Guard Duty

The one noteworthy moment of the entire three months was my first guard duty. We were required to wear freshly starched fatigues for this "honor." By starched, the Army meant able to stand alone, even without your lower body in them. You had to force your feet through the pant legs little by little to pry them apart. Cardboard would have felt better against your skin.

Now, I was out of freshly starched fatigues, which meant that the Non-Commissioned Officers (NCOs: Sergeants) who owned me for that season would have just cause to hurt me. In desperation, I threw myself on the mercy of another trainee, who I barely knew, but who was about my size. He lent me a pair of his fatigue pants.

Late that night, those same NCOs dropped me off at the outhouse-sized guard shack by a deserted warehouse, all by my lonesome. I was required to walk around the fenced perimeter continually throughout the night. Each circuit took about half an hour.

Later, I found out that one of our guards-in-training discovered an open M-48 tank at his post, crawled inside, and slept the whole time. Since I was among the young and dumb, and still severely conscientious, of course I faithfully walked my perimeter all night.

Armed with an empty M-14 rifle on my shoulder, I marched around guarding what-from-whom I never knew, but I was scared enough as if it were the real thing. So scared, in fact, that I failed to judge the bursting point of my bladder. 'Just one more time around,' I told myself, 'then I'll find a needy bush.'

On that last promised circuit, however, I heard something! I anxiously lowered my M-14 and fixed my bayonet to the muzzle. Finally, I spotted the culprit: a loose shutter blowing in the chilly breeze. As I relaxed, and my muscles wriggled free of panic's grip, so did my bladder. It sounded the 20-second breached floodgate alarm!

Now, the Army is big on layers. My gloves were thin leather shells that fastened by a cinch over thick wool inserts, and my button-fly pants were over my long underwear, over boxer shorts.

Did I mention they were button-fly pants? With gloves? And multiple layers of G.I.-issued clothing?

So, after I missed the 20-second warning—by a mere minute and a half—I wet my pants . . . which weren't actually mine.

"I'm sorry," I told the unfortunate soldier who was about my size and lent his clothes to guys he hardly knew who had social problems, "but I wet your pants." Then I handed the starched, stained remnants to the soldier. He never said anything; in fact, he never spoke to me again. He just looked at me with a peculiar hint of betrayal in his eyes and took back his pants.

And that ended our friendship and the only guard duty I ever pulled—and the only time I wet myself—in my three-year Army career.

Chapter 4: Medical Training

Medical Training at Fort Sam Houston, Texas, during July and August, was hot and humid, night and day. It was a good prelim for Vietnam, in a number of ways: all year around Nam was too hot and too humid. The U.S. military had developed the knack of choosing only the most extreme locales—freezing cold or blistering heat—to fight a war. But war, by its very nature, dictates extremes—in sacrifice, courage, and attitude—so why not in weather?

In this narrative, I won't repeat myself by mentioning how hot and sticky and wet we were at any one time. They are a constant in Vietnam and jungle warfare. Stand in any one place in Vietnam too long and you leave some kind of puddle . . . of rain . . . of sweat . . . of blood. A moving target is always the hardest to hit. Keep moving for your life. Keep moving or die. Death catches up with you when you stop moving. As legendary pitcher Satchel Paige once said, "Never look back; something might be gaining on you."

Another constant in the Army and Vietnam is profanity. Most accounts of war that I've read use it—overuse it—for shock value. I find it more distracting than anything else, like gratuitous nudity or sex in a poorly plotted movie. There's a point where it becomes white noise. If I included all the swearing that went on, this book would be significantly longer, but not measurably better.

July 16

At the end of this two weeks of Leadership Training, we'll be forwarded to the Medical Training Area to await the arrival of 600 new Medical Trainees, most of whom are Conscientious Objectors and are appointed to Medical Training. Few of them are volunteers, unlike most of the Trainee Leaders. It should be interesting.

Their Basic Combat Training is only six weeks and excludes rifle, hand-to-hand combat, and bayonet training.

We leaders (Platoon Guides and Squad Leaders) have special privileges—no KP, no details, no guard duty, 72-hour passes every weekend, and special maroon helmets that we wear with medical and leadership insignias on them.

We have our first inspection tomorrow (one every day). Please do not send any food—there is no place for it during

inspections and it's too hot and muggy for it anyway. I haven't eaten any of the regular meals served today—only a bite or two at the PX. Humidity and homesickness are still getting me down.
All for now. Give my love to everybody and God bless.

Brad

For some unknown reason, privy only to Superior Officers, I was pulled out of the normal cycle and subjected to two weeks of Leadership Preparatory Course (LPC) schooling. All this meant is that when my real medical training resumed, I would be an acting platoon sergeant, responsible for marching 30 or so medical misfits to and from classes, administering minor military discipline, assigning barrack duties, and other assorted asinine activities. For my additional trouble and longer hours, I would be first in line to make Private First Class (PFC)—a rather ludicrous distinction since everyone was at least a PFC before going to Vietnam.

For the sake of humiliation, we LPCs were required to wear purple helmets to distinguish us from the rank and file. The rank and file therefore referred to us as "Grape Heads." It was neither a term of endearment nor respect.

Once graduated, I was assigned to the platoon of one Staff Sergeant Owen Fester—a constantly sweating, rotund waste of a man. He was under extreme pressure for being named Top Soldier—when it was obvious to everyone he wasn't—and he passed the pressure on to his LPCs.

"Mens," SSgt. Fester addressed us LPCs in his quarters on a hot Texas afternoon, "Mens, when one of these pups comes to you and says he's in love with some girl he just met in San Anton, don't you believe him. He ain't in love, he's in heat!"

Fester taught me that sergeants are only human, too.

One rare privilege that was granted LPCs came in the form of four walls, two windows, and a door. Rather than sleeping out in the bay in bunks with the platoon, I was granted the rank-has-its-privileges luxury of a room. My room came complete with a built-in friend: Ken Williams.

In the real world, Ken had been a magazine photographer in Chicago. Except for the fact that he liked to wake up in the morning to soul music on my clock radio, which I didn't, and would yank the

22

radio out of the wall and throw it into his locker when I tried to change stations, we got along pretty well.

Since LPCs were supposed to be leaders, we were often called on to demonstrate medical procedures in front of the class. In one such class on inter-muscular injections in the deltoid muscle of the upper arm, I was designated "stuckee" and Ken, "stickee." What I didn't know was that Ken had been goofing off during the instruction phase and failed to pick up the finer points of inserting finer points.

We stood in the middle of the room, surrounded by trainees sitting at tables. I rolled up my sleeve as Ken unwrapped a sterile needle, which he promptly dropped. He made a stutter step to retrieve it, thought again, and reached for a second sterile needle. With some effort, he attached it to the syringe, poked it through the membrane of a small bottle of saline solution, siphoned out a few milliliters of fluid, and then looked at me. His eyes seemed to say, 'You'd better turn away,' which I did.

I expected a prick of pain, which I got, but I didn't anticipate what followed: a chorus of horrified gasps from the audience. I looked down at the site of entry to find the needle, twisted and bent, protruding from my shoulder muscle. I looked at Ken the way Caesar must have looked at Brutus, right after he plunged the dagger home.

"Just pull it out," I heard one of the instructor sergeants say, "and try again." 'Sure,' I thought. 'It's not your arm!' On Ken's second try, and third needle, he succeeded.

"I was busy talking," he admitted later, "instead of listening." 'I was busy bleeding,' I wanted to reply, 'instead of not bleeding.'

September 24
Thought you might like to see this week's training schedule. Last week was probably the most important week, what with injections and intravenous feeding. The ninth and tenth weeks, if anything, are an anticlimax to our training. About the only important classes this week are: Treatment of Battle Casualties, the Medical Proficiency Test (Bandaging and Splints—First Aid) and the Advanced Ward Training Test II (Veni-puncture, Intra-Muscular Injections in the rear, and Bed Patient Care).

Rumor has it that the Vietnam-bound guys may begin special training for the next two weeks (apart from the scheduled program). This would probably be conducted at Camp Bullis, near here.

I'm enclosing post cards of Brook General Hospital and Brackenridge Park.

All for now.

Love, Brad

After ten weeks, I concluded that the Surgeon General should slap a big red warning label on Medical Training. It can definitely be hazardous to your health.

Besides death by a thousand pricks at the hands of your co-trainees, the Army also had what it called the "Confidence Course." In Basic Training, this might consist of charging up a hill firing live ammo at pop-up silhouettes. Or it could mean crawling underneath live machine gun fire while sadists with stripes touched off pits filled with TNT all around you. In Army vernacular, "Confidence" evidently translates into "Fear."

The Club Med Training version of this Fear Course began with simulated wounded on a simulated battlefield, replete with the sounds of automatic weapons fire and the occasional concussion grenade. We even sported rubber, tissue wounds designed for arms, legs, chests, and abdomens. I had one strapped to my right forearm. A hidden tube even pumped simulated blood—when it worked. In the grandest traditions of theater in the park, I screamed my lungs out in pain as two of my Medic trainees tried to locate and dress my concealed gunshot wound.

Now the "Course" part of it all entered the fray. We numbered off one through five down the ranks. The first four were designated stretcher bearers; the fortunate fifth man became the casualty.

Once in our new five-man groups, we secretly renumbered ourselves so that the smallest, a.k.a. lightest, man became the casualty. Then it was off to the races, literally. Whereas win, place, and show garnered no tangible rewards, dropping the patient anywhere along the obstacle course meant going back to the beginning and starting all over again.

Dutifully, we carried our hero over hills and down gullies, through sand pits, and around boulders and trees, until we encountered a seven-foot-high wire fence. A diagram called for us to lift the patient above our heads until the front of the stretcher rested on the top of the fence. Then numbers 1 and 2 climbed up and over. Once they regained their positions on the other side, we would lift and move the stretcher forward until the other half rested on the top and numbers 3 and 4 could climb over. Once they regained their places, we lowered the stretcher and continued on our exhausting journey.

At least, that was the plan. In practice, as we struggled to lift and hold our hero above our heads, the litter suddenly became magically lighter. This was followed by a heavy "Thud!" from the gravel to one side of us and the sound of a man in pain. We had dropped our patient on his side from a height of seven feet. He probably really was a patient now. He continued to moan.

"Shut up, Man!" we whispered in unison. "Get back on the stretcher! Hurry up!"

As one, and with preservation as our purpose, we scanned for sergeants. Coast clear. We would not be going back to square one. On our second attempt, we cleared the high bar without executing the "Fosbury Flop."

At last, our final obstacle flowed serenely in front of us: a 50-foot-wide river. Always one for innovating on the run, the Army had devised a way of lashing four stretchers together and sheathing them in tent halves to create a serviceable—albeit temporary—raft.

"Lookie at that, will ya," cried Tom.

"Shucks," said Huck, "them Army fellers ain't as dumb as pea-green paint after all."

As we stood in line waiting our turn to board the U.S.S. Army's Armada, one proud Viking craft and its stalwart crew of five reached the half-way point across the stream. Then, as it paused, its canvas sides unfurled like some majestic flag, water rushed in, and it sank. The crew of soldier-sailors was left up to their armpits in water . . . as rolls of on-shore laughter sounded "Taps" in their memory.

Chapter 5: Over There

Our ticket to Vietnam was a C-141 "Starlifter." We entered the four-engine jet transport through the tailgate where we stowed our duffel bags in a huge cargo net attached to the ramp door. There were no windows. Once inside, I became disoriented, failing to notice our seats faced to the rear of the plane. When the plane took off, and what I imagined to be the nose dipped down when it should have pointed up, I thought we had bought it for sure.

Our only stop was Wake Island, a milestone in World War II reduced to a stepping stone for Vietnam. It was bleak and barren; nothing worth dying for that I could see. It looked like only the seagull dung was keeping it afloat.

When we landed at Tan Son Nhut AFB near Saigon and they lowered the tailgate, the heat and humidity of Vietnam hit us like a convection oven. At the staging area of Bien Hoa, I spent a horrible week—a second week actually, after a similar one in Oakland while waiting to deploy to Vietnam—of pulling KP, filling sandbags, and every other degrading duty the Army could muster. Finally, I got my orders for the 1st Cav.

I arrived in country on October 26, 1966, just in time for both the Northeast Monsoon season and Operation Thayer II. Thayer was such a hit at the box office that they evidently made a sequel. At the time, the 1st Cav patrolled a 15,000-square-mile region from the Cambodian border to the South China Sea with names like Crow's Foot, Happy Valley, An Loa Valley, VC Valley, the Crescent, and Bong Son.

Though I was scared, I felt prepared. I had applied myself in Medical Training. I was the highest scoring LPC in our cycle. I knew my stuff because I knew it might well mean life or death for one of my patients.

I also felt I knew the VC better than most of the rank-and-file G.I.s around me. Mao, I read your book! One passage in particular stuck in my mind:

What is basic guerrilla strategy? Guerrilla strategy must be based primarily on alertness, mobility, and attack. It must be adjusted to the enemy situation, the terrain, the existing lines of communication, the relative strengths, the weather, and the situation of the people.

In guerrilla warfare, select the tactic of seeming to come from the east and attacking from the west; avoid the solid, attack the hollow; attack; withdraw; deliver a lightning blow, seek a lightning decision. When guerrillas engage a stronger enemy, they withdraw when he advances; harass him when he stops; strike him when he is weary; pursue him when he withdraws. In guerrilla strategy, the enemy's rear, flanks, and other vulnerable spots are his vital points, and there he must be harassed, attacked, dispersed, exhausted and annihilated." (*Mao Tse-Tung on Guerrilla Warfare*, page 46. Copyright © 1961 by Praeger Publishers, New York.)

The division's base camp at An Khe had all the ambiance of an overgrown prison. A peak with a huge 1st Cav patch dominated the landscape like some kind of lighthouse from green Hell. A smaller patch rested on a lower peak nearby. It was one of the scariest places I've ever been—and it was only the *rear* area!

In stark contrast, LZ Hammond at Phu Cat was all sand and no land. It looked naked and vulnerable as if a dozen Mama Sans with brooms could sweep us into the South China Sea. And it had a pronounced sleazy feel to it . . . like living in a vacant lot outside of Tijuana. I'd never felt so alone, so isolated.

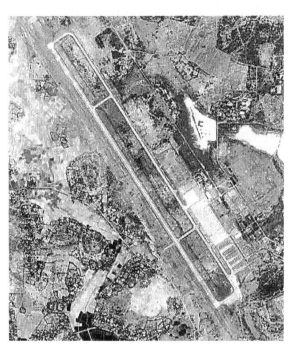

LZ Hammond at Phu Cat via satellite—a much better view than I had from the ground.

Hammond was desolate in other ways as well. I had always had problems making new friends. Maybe it was me, maybe not. All I know is that after nearly a month, I hardly knew anyone.

I shared a tent with the other C Troop Medic, Doc Stone. He was more predator than person, as cold and flinty as his name. Stone and I were polar opposites; but he was older, had been there and back, and so I listened to him. What choice did I have?

"Do you want to hear a letter from a girl I've been seeing?" he said one evening before lights out.

"Sure," I said. What else did I have to do?

"OK, she's pregnant, so she writes, 'Stoney, when the child is old enough, do you want me to tell him who his father is?' " Then he laughed, a laugh that echoed like his heart was at the bottom of some deep, slimy-walled well.

We alternated days going out. At first, he got all the good actions on his days. He told me about one patrol:

"We were sweeping villages this morning and Capt. Blue gave me these two gooks to guard. One was wounded, so I overdosed him with two syrettes of morphine. He died. The other one was in front of me, his hands tied behind his back, going down a trail. I waited until we turned a bend and no one was behind us. Then I shot him in the back of the head." Same vacant, echoing laughter.

A minute later, Capt. Blue doubled up his 6-foot-3-inch frame and crouched his way into our tent. "So, the Doc can save a life or take a life," he said to Stone.

"Sir?" Stone said.

"You know what I'm talking about: today—the prisoners."

"No, Sir. One died of his wounds and the other tried to escape. I had no choice."

The Captain looked at him with his face tilted to one side, nodded, and then left.

In November, I entrusted Stone with several silk scarves I had bought in Phu Cat for my mom and sisters. I boxed them up and handed him a buck's worth of G.I. scrip for postage. My family never received them for Christmas.

That was Doc Stone. When I got there, that's what C Troop thought a Medic was like. They were taking few prisoners back then, none wounded, and prisoners are a key ingredient in the recipe for an effective Recon unit.

Save your friends and send the rest to Hell. Is that what it took to be hardcore? Is that what it took to be accepted by the others? Or is that what you become in time—what I would become in time—after the war was finished remaking me from the inside out? I didn't know.

October 30

This being Sunday, I went to church at 1:00. The services are held in the improvised movie theater. Seats are unserviceable

29

helicopter blades and the floor is dirt (though this afternoon it was mostly mud and running water). The sermon was drowned out by monsoon rains, but prayer was still perceptible.

Most likely, I'll have my two or three days of experience with the M-16 and helicopter tactics Monday and Tuesday, October 31 and November 1. My first combat patrol will be sometime next week with probably C Troop of the 1st Squadron, 9th Cavalry Regiment of the 1st Cavalry Division. They have the best record here for longevity of their personnel, so I'm in good hands.

I've been spending some time boning-up on the drugs I'll need to know. Incidentally, I'm taking the place of a Specialist 5 (E-5) who is going home.

In the next few letters, I'll send you several 1st Cav patches to dye green and send back. Thanks.

Love, Brad

Post Script

I didn't tell my family that the helicopter blades were "unserviceable" because they were riddled with bullet holes, and the "best record for longevity of personnel" was someone's idea of a joke. Welcome to the 1st Cav!

I remember sitting in the Mess Tent at Thanksgiving, when something right out of the movies happened: a guy with a guitar began to sing. His improvisation was to the tune of the "Ballad of the Green Berets":

"Here I am in Vietnam,
Hiding from the Viet Cong.
Seems like just the other day,
I got my letter from LBJ.

He said, 'Son, I'm 'fraid to say,
Gonna send your butt far, far away.
You may scream and you may cry,
But you can't hide from the FBI . . . ."

That's how a lot of us felt about the war, really felt deep down inside, whether we volunteered or were drafted. I never wrote home about such things. I never wrote home about my first day in combat, either, but I'll never forget it . . . .

Chapter 6: First Contact

We were on Search and Destroy in a grassy, unpopulated valley, a nice place for a picnic if we had been stateside. At one point along the narrow trail, I saw a bamboo stalk jutting from foliage at about shoulder level. I rested my hand on it before we continued.

"Hey, Doc," whispered the unknown soldier behind me as we moved on, "that was a booby trap!"

I looked back at him sheepishly. My expression said, 'Sorry, I'm new.'

I was also new enough not to bring along any C rations. Capt. Blue told the other guys to give me what they didn't want, so my first—and potentially last—supper consisted of canned ham-me-downs.

Then it happened! "Pop! Pop! Pop!" While I was busy following the guy in front of me, C Troop spotted an ambush and strategically circled around to come up behind it. We caught one VC cold, and left him that way, forever.

Kneeling on the trail to use the elephant grass for concealment, my face was a scant two feet from his face for what seemed like an eternity. For him, it was. The top of his head was gone, sheared clean off, like the missing lid to a cookie jar. His yellow, pureed brains looked like tapioca pudding, a dish I've never stomached since. His eyes were wide open and empty looking, as if he couldn't believe he was dead. By his smooth features, I took him to be about 15 years old. Another soldier, seasoned to the expressions of death, said he was more like 30.

Other than my best friend Jim in high school who committed suicide our freshman year, I had never seen a dead man. As I was forced to step over him leaning down, I said out loud, "I'm sorry. I'm really sorry." I didn't care who heard me.

As the shadows lengthened, I could sense a growing urgency in the young men around me. They were scared too, not of the dark, but of the small dark men we hunted. We were on their turf now, on their time; we were the hunted now.

With nightfall, the VC lit camp fires at intervals on the tops of the hills. Soon, these funeral pyres from Hell surrounded us.

In any other war, this first combat might very well have been my last. But this was Vietnam, a helicopter war, and we were the 1st Air Cavalry Division! With only running lights visible that made their great blades vanish in the night, the choppers looked like sharks cruising the inky depths above our heads. Only these weren't predators, they were answers to prayer. That night, I discovered the sheer bliss of being airlifted out of danger. In minutes we had regained the high ground. I watched the ring of fire drop away below us, a relic of wars gone by, now little more than a poor Fourth of July joke. Surrounding the 1st Cav was like trying to bottle the sky—and we owned the sky. The Commies would never beat us!

Back at Phu Cat and LZ Hammond the cooks kept the mess tent open late to serve us a hot meal. I stood in line, glad to be alive, while they piled my tray high. As I carried it outside into the night, I passed a row of officers' tents. Bought in the States and handed down from officer to officer, these canvas cathedrals were mansions compared to the pup tent halves that we enlisted men snapped together. The officer digs were tall enough so you could actually stand up inside like a real person. They also had something else our tents didn't: guide wires.

One reached out from the dark, hit me thigh high, and sent me sprawling. I landed atop tray and meal, mashed potatoes filling my .45 pistol holster.

Voices from the tent followed my fall, "Did you hear that? What was it?"

I hurried off into the shadows before they could come out— to find a private place for a private to cry.

Chapter 7: The Enemy

In the Vietnam War, the Communists offered us a two-for-one sale; two enemies for the price of one: the Viet Cong (VC) and the North Vietnam Army (NVA).

The VC we called "Charlie." It was more than a name derived from the U.S. Army radio call letters for VC, Victor Charlie. It mirrored the contempt we held for them; a contempt born of fear. During the day they hid, disguised as rice farmers. At night or wrapped in an invisible cloak of jungle, they attacked, and then disappeared again. It was like trying to catch Casper the Unfriendly Ghost.

The NVA, on the other hand, were a force to be reckoned with—as in dead reckoning. Out of respect, we called them "Mr. Charles." They fought in regiment-sized units—thousands of highly trained soldiers armed with the latest automatic weapons. They came looking for us, with both attitude and a lot of latitude. And they were packing: AK-47 assault rifles that fired at 600 rpm, RPG-7 grenade launchers that could penetrate 22 inches of hardened armor; the works. And that was just on the ground. In the air, over North Vietnam, they flew MiG-21 jet fighters at more than twice the speed of sound. Ringing Hanoi, our B-52 heavy bombers and fighter-bombers faced the most formidable air defense system in history, comprised of Russian Surface-to-Air Missiles (SAMs) and anti-aircraft guns.

Air-dropped propaganda leaflet depicting the 1St Cav stomping on the NVA.

Call them Charlie, or Charles, or something derogatory, it didn't matter. When you went up against them, inside your secret room of the shakes, deep down inside your quivering gut, you called them "Sir." Give them an AK-47 and they were huge, Mt. Everest huge. When you faced them across a rice paddy or in the jungle, it was always feasible that they had your number, crisply folded and creased, tucked just inside a black silken pocket.

And beside those rice paddies and jungles, they also lived across the street. Their terrorist tactics accounted for 33,000 deaths and 58,000 kidnappings during the war; foreshadowing of the Taliban of another time.

Two enemies: one hit-and-run, the other we wanted to run from. Together they cut and slashed at us like a two-edged dagger.

There was a third blade to contend with, however, one with a serrated edge that left a deep and jagged scar—one that never really healed. And it came at us from behind, from our backs . . . from back home, to be exact.

The Tet Offensive of 1968 has been called a turning point of the war. Considering we inflicted 45,000 KIAs—compared to the 1,000 dead the enemy dealt us in return—it should have been scored a clear and telling victory in our column. The well-coordinated offensive turned into a crippling rout for the Communist forces in the South after we killed half of them. Yet, back home it was reported as a defeat for the U.S.

If the same yardstick had been applied to the Normandy landings of June 6, 1944, would that have been seen as a defeat, too? Would the American public have given up fighting the Axis powers and Hitler, like it gave up on stopping North Vietnam and Ho Chi Minh? When LBJ pulled the plug on his tenure two months after Tet because he was afraid to run against Bobby Kennedy, the freedom baby went down the drain with the bath water. Pillars of the press dubbed the war unwinnable. The people believed and the moment was lost. In Vietnam, the misperception may well have denied us victory at Tet and final victory in the war.

And it gets worse. Somewhere along the line as the war was perceived more and more as a lost cause, the finger of blame reared its ugly digit. And somewhere along the line, the American people got the idea it was our fault, those who fought.

The gruesome scenes of My Lai helped, coupled with TV and movie depictions of Vietnam vets as wanton, sadistic killers. Maybe writers, producers, and directors thought we should be inwardly tormented about losing the war. Whatever the case, we were unjustly singled out as the real villains.

Even as recently as the 1990s, that image has persisted. I recall the high-ranking Clinton staff member who during a TV interview exclaimed that the reason we lost the Vietnam War was because "we didn't send our best and our brightest." Far from being fired or even reprimanded, she barely received even a cuff on the nose with a rolled up newspaper. No doubt, her opinion was widely held within the alabaster halls of power at that time. President Clinton did cut the military by 40 percent during his tenure, so we couldn't effectively fight another Vietnam War—or any other war for that matter. I still have vivid images of mothers, in full National Guard uniforms, saying good bye to their young children as they went off to the second Gulf War. They and their families paid the price for those cuts; for the Clintons' disdain for all things military.

"We didn't send our best and our brightest". . . Funny, but when I was in Nam I thought we were the best, just maybe not the brightest. Of course, I'm defining "bright" as those who look after number one as their top priority. If the brightest stayed in school and dodged the draft, that wasn't us either. If the brightest valued their own lives and freedoms over the millions of people unable to defend themselves against Communist enslavement, I guess that wasn't us, too.

But if we weren't exactly the brightest when it came to playing it safe and cool, I still think what we tried to do over there puts us right on top of the humanity heap with the best. And if that's what our troops tried to do in Afghanistan and Iraq, then we're in good company—the best company. Personally, I wouldn't have it any other way.

Chapter 8: Charles Roberts

In this corner: Southpaw, Southside Roberts!

Charles Roberts and I had an interesting, though "Rocky" relationship. Charles came over with me on the plane as a replacement. He was from Chicago and had fought Archie Moore Division as a middleweight. His Southside accent and a tendency to garble his words—either from where he grew up, or a few too many punches, or both—struck me as funny. I made fun of him once, quoting Marlon Brando's "On the Waterfront" punch-drunk character: "I coulda had class. I coulda been a contender. I coulda been somebody." After my one-man show, Charles really did want to strike me funny; how funny, I didn't realize until one day in the field.

I was plugging the holes my friends had made in a VC, not knowing Charles was keeping a close watch. Suddenly, he leaned over my shoulder and snarled, "I don't like the way you're treating him. If I'm ever wounded and you treat me like that, I'll kill you!"

I continued working, but replied, "Charles, if I ever have to treat you and you even look like you might try to kill me, I'll fill you so full of morphine you'll never wake up. And they won't be able to prove a thing."

After that, we became friends, good friends in fact. You might say we had come to a mutual understanding. Of course, I was bluffing, and I imagined he was too; but after that I never made fun of him again, just in case. In Nam, the difference between a bluff and a snuff is just the slightest touch on a trigger.

With our new understanding, I began to appreciate him more. In one action, Charles was on point crossing a paddy when his Asian namesake, "Charlie," opened up. The first round hit Charles in the plastic stock of his M-16. Now, in previous wars this would have been no big deal, especially with wooden stocks. The M-16, however, is so designed that the bolt travels from the breech back through the stock at recoil. The spring inside the stock then drives the bolt back again reloading another round into the chamber. So, busted stock, busted rifle, busted butt.

Knowing this, in boxing terms, Charles took a dive; he went into the tank. He dropped like a sack of potatoes and didn't budge through the rest of the firefight. The VC thought he was dead, so they didn't shoot at him again. It saved his life. Doc Shore, my alternate that day, knew he was faking it; and since we don't make house calls for shattered weapons, Charles' act may have saved the Doc's life as well.

When it was over, Charles got up, dusted himself off, and boarded the chopper. Charles was cool, Chicago Southside cool.

On another operation a few days later, the Brass up above called down with orders to waste a water buffalo. The guys obliged with a volley of M-16 fire into its side. It looked irritated and began to chase Smitty into a hooch and out the other side—through a bamboo and palm-branch wall. I realized their 55-grain M-16 .22-caliber rounds weren't penetrating, so to protect them and put the beast out of its misery, I pulled out my trusty, rusty .45 automatic pistol and thumped a round into its side. It went down like . . . well, like a wounded water buffalo. When it got up again, to my surprise, I aimed for its head this time and put it down permanently. It was my first confirmed kill.

The next operation, I would know how it felt . . . .

Chapter 9: A Scar is Born

December 1, 1966, The Battle of Bong Son . . . You won't find it in the record books, in any collection of great battles. It didn't turn the tide of a war, or free a people, or win a peace. The only ones who remember it are those who were there: the 1st Air Cav. "December 1st," they would say thereafter, in hushed, reverent tones. It became the stuff of legend, like some great, gray benchmark that all other battles, past and future, would be measured against. It was a yardstick of carnage, the worst nightmare of any soldier, something to look back on and say, "If I made it through December 1st, I can make it through anything." Even if it wasn't true, somehow it helped, just a little.

In the best traditions of the worst fiction, the night of November 30th was dark and rainy. C Troop had spent a boring day—the kind of day a soldier lives for—conducting Search and Destroy missions through the villages of the Bong Son plain. This affluent, rice-rich region was a favorite of Charlie. The amiable populace was all-too willing to aid their hometown heroes. And if they weren't all that willing, Charlie persuaded them by shooting the random villager. That left us the role of the Sheriff of Nottingham and his medieval goons, in hopeless pursuit of the stealthy Robin and his merry band. The only physical difference in this analogy is that we wore the green uniforms and they sported black silk loungewear. "You know," I would say later, "those VC beat us in their pajamas."

I had only been in the field for three weeks—a week of that grounded with an ear infection—so the heavily armed teenagers flanking me were strangers. Only later would I enter into their gang mentality, once I had proven myself. For now, in both name and disposition, they were a mystery to me. All I knew is that I needed them, so I never let the man in front of me out of my sight.

Tales of faraway wars, wasted lives, and young men braver than their years. Photo courtesy of Sgt. Tong, ARVN Interpreter.

Toward dusk, we set up an OP (Observation Post) in an old abandoned Catholic church. No one took off their helmets as we entered through a doorless side portal. It really wasn't a church anymore anyway, since half the roof was missing, along with all the people. Like the finger game you played as a kid: "Here's the church, here's the steeple, open the door . . . where are all the people?" Amputated? Cut off by the war? MIA? WIA? KIA?

As my eyes adjusted to the light, the first thing I saw staring back at me were garishly painted icons bracketing the altar. Untouched, for the Vietnamese were very superstitious, they guarded the gutted edifice. Unblinking, silent as death, they stood, soldiers of another cause, another war. If they had won their battle for hearts and minds, we might not be here . . . wet, lonely, and forgotten.

During the day, we had detained two young girls, high-school age. Now our Vietnamese interpreter, Sgt. Coung (we called him "Cong"), nervously spoke with the captain about their safety. He had seen the coyote-hungry looks of some of the troop and feared for the girls. Capt. Blue, a family man himself, assured him their honor would be upheld during the night. It was. Some of the guys even shared their C-rations with them.

Capt. Blue broke open a Claymore Mine to extract just enough of the C-4 plastic explosive to cook his dinner. He always did; he liked his little pleasures. He opened the cans with a church key (fittingly), stuck his bayonet through one side of the can as a handle, lit the C-4, and cooked his ham steak over the slow-burning flames.

I ate my pork and beans cold, the way the Army intended. Then I found a dry spot on the dirt floor for the night. Taking a page from the Captain's manual of gracious living, I used my aid bag as a pillow. It beat using my helmet. For a night light, I put my loaded .45 automatic pistol on my stomach. I had traded my rifle for the handgun back in An Khe. I thought it would be more of a defensive weapon than the offensive M-16—making it less likely for me to take a life. After all, I reasoned, I was a Medic; our motto was "To Conserve Fighting Strength," not "Kill Your Quota." I was supposed to save lives, not add to the body count.

Vietnam taught me how to sleep. The more you slept over there, the less time you were actually in country. Sleep was release; escape. Sometimes I even slept on the helicopter—no doors and 100-mile-per-hour winds screaming a foot away—going to and coming back from a mission. It was a gift from my dad, and I made the most of it. He could excuse himself from a boring dinner party, take a 10-minute "power nap," and return refreshed, like he'd never been away.

Nam taught me another nighttime trick—how to sleep with my eyes open. Fear has that effect. Of course, I didn't realize I was wide-eyed all night at the time. I only found out much later in the hospital when a shocked Orderly thought I had died in my sleep and nervously tried to revive me.

At midnight, I had already been out for close to four hours, when my peace was shattered by machine gun fire! Still lying face up, I instinctively pulled my .45 from my stomach and drew a bead on the first shadow in range. I tracked it just long enough to recognize the shape as a "friendly," one of our own guys! After I started breathing again, I promised myself to keep my weapons holstered from now on.

As suddenly as it began, it was over. The lone VC who crossed our path lay dead in the dark. "Never knew what hit him?" Oh, he *knew* all right, but not for long. By morning, rigor mortis had contorted him into the fetal position. 'He went out the same way he came into the world,' I thought. 'Only this time, his mother couldn't make it.'

Lesson #1: War is demeaning.

December 1st picked up where November 30th left off. We ate another meal of "Cs" and took another little walk in the rain. Along the way, we released the two girls, trading them for two local men of military age. We tied their hands behind their backs to take them to An Khe later for interrogation. Maybe they were VC, maybe not.

"Doc, you got anything for tired feet?" Benson asked.

"Retreads?" I replied, trying to make a joke. There was no cure for tired feet, not in this world.

It wasn't the funniest reply; stand-up comedy is hard in fatigues. Nam is a tough room, but he smiled anyway. If I'd had more time to think, I might have said, "Try rotating your feet every 5,000 miles."

At about 10:00 am, we got the word from on high (one of the Huey B gunships escorting us) that the "slicks" (Huey D troop helicopters) would be picking us up in an hour. We'd be returning to Phu Cat for dry clothes and a hot meal, and probably the rest of the day off. You couldn't ask for better news.

The locals were particularly friendly. The kids actually smiled at us as we walked by. I smiled back and even waved.

Lesson #2: In war, you're either bored to death or scared to death. There is no in-between. The first one just kills you a little slower.

By 10:45 am, we were hurrying through the last village, Phu Huu 2, when one of our gunships radioed down that it had spotted "some guy in a hole" in the woods running parallel to our path.

Reluctantly, we left the well-worn trail to check it out. It all seemed routine enough . . . probably just a stray farmer or a kid . . . no sweat.

But it was something to sweat about! Hidden in that placid little woods lurked row upon row of zig-zag trenches, spider holes, and earth-and-log bunkers. And inside them bristled the automatic rifles and machine guns of 300 North Vietnam Army troops. We were walking headlong into an ambush!

"Crack! Crack! Crack! Crack!" The deadly report of AK-47s sent men and boys scrambling for cover.

Confused and afraid, I looked to Sgt. Cain, the John Wayne of the troop, for some kind of reassurance. I was devastated by what I saw. There was the indestructible sergeant, red hair and mustache flying, spinning like a top from the impact of round after round! He finally landed in a broken heap behind a tree, with his back to the enemy, 30 yards in front of me.

As I watched, his mouth contorted and spat out a single word whose impact I would never forget: "Medic!"

In my mind I said, 'If this was for real, I'd use that tree straight ahead for cover, then cut across the opening to his tree.'

Before I realized it, that's what I was doing—for real. Using the woods for cover, I narrowly managed to snake my way through a storm of automatic weapons fire. Later, Rowdy told me, "Doc, the bullets were hitting all around your feet the whole way. I don't know how you made it."

Lesson #3: War is a matter of the mundane and the miraculous.

Just as I reached the sergeant's tree, three or four rounds hit the sides sending bark ricocheting into my face. The pieces peppered me with such force that I mistook them for bullets. For one long, breathless moment I stopped to feel my face for what I thought would be the shredded remains of my identity: eyes, nose, mouth, cheeks. To my relief, all were intact.

Now, I turned my attention to the sergeant. As I stared, he pulled up his blood-soaked green undershirt. "Doc, I'm all messed up," he said, or words to that effect. I gazed in disbelief at the sight of another human being with "real live" bullet holes through his chest. Three were evident: two through his left lung and another dangerously near his heart. I reasoned it must have hit at an angle, shattering his sternum. A straight-on hit would have killed him.

I fumbled with a first-aid dressing, all the while never believing the sergeant would live out the next minute. Training hadn't prepared me for this and the movies lied—you can be hit in the chest and still live. Suddenly, his eyes grew wide and lidless, and I thought my deathwatch had ended. Then I realized he was looking at something behind us.

As the hairs bristled on the back of my neck, I turned to see what he was gawking at in such fear. A trail of machine gun bullets was stitching a lethal seam straight for us! In the confusion of smoke and trees, one of our own gunships was strafing us!

Sgt. Cain lurched backwards against the tree, while I crouched into a ball. One round hit the ground between our legs and another struck the tree just above Cain's head. We had somehow found that elusive middle ground between rounds.

Now, the reality of the situation broke over me like the crest of a tidal wave: move six inches to either side of the tree and I was dead meat; stay behind the tree and one of our own helicopters would chalk us up. And all the while the sergeant lay dying.

Out of the burnt-gunpowder haze, I could hear the haunting cries of other men: "Medic! Medic! Medic!" I began to crack under the strain. Panic enveloped me. My tortured emotions screamed for release. Even my senses began to fail me. I watched another trooper throw a grenade that careened off a branch short of its intended target. When it exploded close by, I heard nothing.

Certain that death was imminent, I began to pray, "God, get ME out of here!" Nothing. Too many years looking for God in too many wrong places had led me to this dead-end street. Even though my mother embarked on my spiritual education at an early age, I only knew facts about God. I had never met Him personally.

Then I realized how selfish my prayer had been, concerned only with my own skin. I looked at the dying sergeant and, for the first time in my life, I forgot about myself. I prayed a different kind of prayer.

"God, forget about me. Just do something for Sgt. Cain. Even if helping him costs me my own life, it's OK."

Suddenly, this seemed like the right thing to do, so I leveled with God even more. "I'm so frozen with fear that I can't even move. If You mean for me to help him, You will have to do it through me. In fact, take my life, You can have it from now on."

At that instant, a peace I had never known before flooded my consciousness. I actually felt a Presence come over me. I knew, without a doubt, that Jesus Christ had entered my heart!

I was no longer frozen with fear and I knew that no matter what happened to me—live or die—it would be all right.

Still, the sergeant was dying. I knew that if he didn't reach a hospital soon, the blood filling his chest cavity, between his diaphragm and his lungs, would suffocate him.

"I need help," I yelled to the soldier behind the tree six feet to my left. "We've got to get him out of here."

PFC Rowdy looked at me for a moment as if I was crazy before deciding to commit himself to the same asylum. Then he grabbed the straps on his shoulders and threw off the radio he was carrying.

At that same time, Pvt. Jorge Martinez crawled up under fire to help his wounded squad leader and friend. It was a miracle he made it at all. They both joined me behind Cain's tree.

"Wait for the gunships to make a run on the enemy's positions to keep their heads down," yelled Capt. Blue from behind the tree to our right, "then make a run for it." No sooner had he finished his sentence, then limbs, leaves, and dirt started flying to our front.

The Olympics never saw a faster start! I carried Cain by the ankles, while Martinez and Rowdy interlocked their hands to support him chair-fashion. He was in too much pain to be carried under the arms.

Sprinting through the underbrush, it looked as if we might escape without a scratch. 'We're gonna make it! We're gonna make it!' I shouted inside my head. Then suddenly, I heard a sickening "splat" like something piercing a soaked sponge.

A warm, oozing sensation trickled down my right arm. Feeling no pain, I thought it must be the sergeant bleeding from a new wound. When we were a safe distance from the scene of the ambush, I shouted, "We've got to put him down! He's hit again. We've got to put him down!"

47

As we leaned down, however, all the grip left my right hand. I looked at my sleeve. It was soaked with blood—my blood!

Lesson #4: You are *NOT* faster than a speeding bullet!

Thoughts of losing my arm—and my longed-for career as a commercial artist—assaulted my mind. Reason told me I should hate the Communists for doing this to me, but I didn't. Instead, the only words out of my mouth were, "Father, forgive them for they don't know what they are doing."

It was just as if someone else had spoken from within me; so I repeated the words to make them my own, "Father, forgive them for they don't know what they are doing." Only later did I realize that they were among Jesus' last words on the cross.

When I rolled up my sleeve, I discovered only two neat little holes, one where the bullet had entered and a slightly larger one where it had exited. Martinez tore the plastic sleeve and paper envelope from a dressing I gave him and unwound the ties. He helped me wrap my arm.

Sgt. Haskett's squad came over to help. They "appropriated" a door from one of the hooches and put Cain on it.

I still wasn't feeling any pain, but I thought I should shoot up with morphine just the same, just in case I did later. Besides, it was a legitimate excuse to try it out. I popped off the protective plastic tube and pushed in the plunger to break the inner seal, all with one hand. Then I stuck the needle its full inch and a half into the deltoid muscle of my right arm and squeezed.

"You hit, too, Doc?" said Haskett.

"Yeah, Sarge," I answered. I might have said something more memorable, but I started seeing big spots. I sat down, and then laid down, letting my helmet roll off my head. Blood rushed back to my brain; enough to keep me from blacking out.

One of our "Fighter Red" gunships swooped down to pick up wounded; C Troop never used "Dust Off" Med Evac choppers. Haskett's squad loaded Cain, door and all, first, and then helped me in. I had lost too much blood to stay, and with only one working arm, I didn't resist.

Lesson #5: Hero is a four-letter word.

Chapter 10: Evac

When the chopper took off with abandon, I flew off my seat and nearly out of the open door. C Troop choppers left non-essentials like doors back at the base. It saved weight. Besides, doors just spoiled the view.

The machine gunner knelt by Sgt. Cain during the 15-minute flight to Qui Nhon. I watched them. The sergeant looked bad, but alive. I prayed for him, then for the rest of the guys left behind. It bothered me that I wouldn't be there to help them. It would bother me for months to come.

Later, C Troop found an NVA mortar team laid out, dead. They had set up their tube to hit our choppers landing to pick up wounded. All we could figure out is that the guy who dropped the first round down the tube didn't move out of the way fast enough. The round must have hit him, exploded, and killed the entire mortar team.

Once at the 85th Evac Hospital along the coast, I was transferred to a stretcher and carried to the ER. Inside, my wound soon took a backseat to my jungle boots, prized by rear-area personnel. They were unceremoniously untied, removed, and soon listed MIA. As another Medic cut off my fatigue shirt, I removed $30 in military scrip from the breast pocket. I had just been paid. I handed it to him for safe keeping. It also disappeared from my personal effects.

They took Cain and some of the others first, naturally. I apologized to Jerry Ware, one of the C Troop guys lying on another table next to me, "I'm sorry I couldn't get to you."

"That's OK, Doc," Ware said. "We knew you were busy with Cain."

When it was finally my turn, they gave me a brachial block—a local anesthetic that left me conscious during surgery. "You've really got a thick neck," said the male nurse as he struggled to find my artery with his needle.

"You would, too," I said, "if you had to wear three pounds of steel pot on your head all day long."

A cloth barrier separated me from what the doctors were doing: filleting my forearm from the bullet entrance hole to the exit hole. I imagined the worst: amputation! One doctor said to another,

"The bullet severed half the ulna nerve, but it missed hitting the major artery and bone by only a millimeter!"

A millimeter—that was the difference between really losing my arm and maybe even bleeding to death. One silly little millimeter made all the difference in the world—at least it did in *my* world.

Lesson #6: War is a matter of millimeters and microseconds.

Following surgery, my still open wound was bandaged. In a couple of days, it would be checked for fragments, and then closed with sutures.

I was wheeled to a ward—the first bed with clean sheets I had seen in two months. They brought me fried chicken and mashed potatoes.

"This is livin', huh?" one of my C Troop ward mates said. I managed a bite of chicken and maybe two of potatoes, before I laid back my head and passed out for the night.

When I woke up, I learned that we had had three Killed In Action (KIA) and eight Wounded In Action (WIA), about half the Troop on December 1st. Capt. Blue had been killed trying to crawl over to retrieve a cleaning rod to unjam his M-16. McNamara and the Pentagon had decided they knew more than gun designer Eugene Stoner. Somewhere along the line, the White House Whiz Kids misrepresented the M-16 to be self-cleaning. At first, they didn't even issue cleaning kits to the troops. They opted to change the gun powder from stick to ball, against Stoner's recommendations. It was cheaper. The dirtier burning ball powder clogged the works. A year later, they changed it back. It had proved too costly.

Benson had been shot through the eye and into his brain. He still moved involuntarily, so one of his buddies kept yelling, "Medic! Medic!" Those were the cries for help I heard while tending to Sgt. Cain.

The third fatality was a crew chief from one of the helicopters. I never knew his name. He only had a week left before rotating home and wanted to experience a firefight from the ground. He did. Now he was under the ground. Words to *live* by: "Stay in the helicopter!"

After helping me carry out Sgt. Cain, Rowdy worked his way back to the front. He got within six feet of a spider hole. An NVA popped up with his AK cracking and shot him through the shoulder. The impact blew Rowdy backwards in a full somersault. His M-16 ended up sticking muzzle first in the mud.

Bethel Smith took shrapnel in one foot. There were three Smiths that day with C Troop: one KIA and two WIA. Doesn't say much for the longevity of us in combat, does it?

Another Cav unit joined the fray that day. A new lieutenant marched them in a line against the NVAs' fixed positions—a tactic that didn't even work in the Civil War. They took 8 KIA and 12 WIA.

Our artillery and chopper strikes were beginning to find the mark—we counted 69 dead—so the remaining 230 or so NVA funneled themselves into an escape tunnel that exited at the river. One of our units saw them coming out, but did nothing about it. Too bad, we might have won the war.

Two days later, I was pushing Smitty in a wheel chair—one-handed—when we saw a familiar, though stooped, figure: Sgt. Cain! He was outside, shirtless, walking. A wad of bandages the size of a dinner roll jutted from the middle of his chest. A dressing and elastic bandage were wrapped around his rib cage. He actually looked glad to see us. I think it was the first time I ever saw him smile; Cain was hard core.

"Hey, Sarge!" Smitty said.

"I didn't expect to see you up and around so soon," I said, trying to sound professional. "How are you doing?"

"OK. The dressings are tight," he said, as he touched the wad in the center of his chest. He held out his hand, "I got hit in the wrist, too." He looked at me. I nodded like I knew it all the time. Must have missed that one.

Then Cain reached into his pajama pocket and pulled out a twisted piece of brass—his Boy Scout-designed, Army-issued belt buckle. One round had hit dead center and ricocheted off. A shot to the gut, along with the damage to his chest, would have killed him for sure.

"They've got me in a ward that's half gooks," he said. "The guy in the bed next to mine is NVA. You know those little paper cups of water they give you with your pills a couple of times a day? Each time I save half of my water, and when the nurses aren't looking, I throw it in his face. The nurses can't figure out why he's wet all the time."

The day they told me I was being flown out to Japan, I stopped at Cain's ward. He was sitting on the edge of a bed talking with a guy from another unit. During our conversation, he turned to the soldier I didn't know and said, "One thing I'll say for the Doc, though, he got me out of there. You know he was shot carrying me out?"

That was it. That was enough. Heroes don't thank other people—that's why they're heroes. Other people thank them. Thank you, Sgt. Cain, Sgt. Haskett, Sgt. Kaneshiro, and Sgt. Samuel. Pros like you keep part-time soldiers like me alive. Thank God for sergeants!

When I began my journalism career in the late '70s, I wrote up a shortened version of the day I was shot for *Power For Living* magazine. After it was published, I got the idea of trying to send it to Sgt. Cain. I knew he lived in Lyons, Kansas, but that was all. I looked up the ZIP code and put his name and my partial address on the envelope, banking on Lyons being a small, rural community where everybody knew everybody. I was right. A week or so later, I received a letter from Cain's mother requesting a dozen copies of the article. She also filled me in on what had happened to her son after December 1st.

Following six months of recuperation in Army hospitals, he returned to the war—for another two years! Finally, the Establishment determined that he had been in Vietnam too long and issued orders to pull him out. On his last scheduled day in the field, however, he stepped on a landmine. The explosion killed the soldier in front of him and the one behind him, but the force just blew him straight up into the air. He lived, but the calf of one of his legs was severely mangled. Eventually, doctors severed the nerves to that leg to relieve the pain. He returned to his farm in Kansas and his family—which according to "Blues" accounts numbered 11 kids!

Chapter 11: Murph and the Movies

Audie Murphy was the single biggest hero to come out of World War II—or any U.S. war for that matter. He killed 240 Axis enemy soldiers and earned more decorations—including the Medal of Honor—than any other American soldier before or since. Give Murph an M-1 Carbine or a Thompson or a .50 machine gun on top of a burning tank, and he was a giant. John Wayne never rode taller or fought braver . . . and he had a script. Later, they gave Murph a script, too.

After World War II, his life took a drastic downturn and Audie ended up living in the back room of a YMCA. What else could he do but write his memoirs.

Hollywood picked up his option, and since Murphy always looked much younger than his years, the Execs decided to star him in their 1952 movie-version of "The Red Badge of Courage," Steven Crane's Civil War classic. Bill Mauldin, the Pulitzer Prize-winning cartoonist from World War II, was also in the cast.

Casting Audie Murphy as Pvt. Henry Fleming, the soldier who runs from his first battle, seems going against type. At least, I thought so when I was younger, before actually going to war. Yet,

Audie played the part with such conviction, such depth, that you would swear he actually lived it. He probably did.

Here's my take on cowards and heroes. They are both equally afraid. The difference is that heroes are more afraid of being cowards, more afraid of letting down their buddies, than they are of being killed themselves.

Hollywood heroes—emotionless, calculating, in control—don't exist in the real world, not in war. A true hero, unlike in the comic books, isn't bulletproof. A real hero risks his life like everyone else and can lose it like everyone else. Otherwise, if there's no danger to him personally, no risk, what is so heroic about him? Real heroes face real danger and die real deaths in real time, otherwise there's nothing real about them.

Finally, Hollywood felt Murph hadn't suffered enough, so they had him relive his war experiences in the movie based on his 1949 best-selling autobiography. After making "To Hell and Back," he said that reenacting the deaths of so many of his friends was one of the hardest things he ever had to do.

Both "To Hell and Back" and "The Red Badge of Courage" are must-see movies. Others—minus Murphy—are: "A Walk in the Sun," "The Story of G.I. Joe," "Battleground," "Patton," "Saving Private Ryan," "Band of Brothers," and "Platoon."

"Platoon," by director Oliver Stone, is the best film on the Vietnam War I've ever seen. Stone served with the 25th Division and later with a Long Range Recon Patrol (LRLP) unit of the 1st Cav. For me, "Platoon" was like a second tour over there. For the most part, I was the Charlie Sheen character "Chris."

Here's some insight I gleaned on Vietnam and war in general from Stone's work. Authors and/or directors (Stone was both) often put hints as to their underlying theme in the names of their characters. Barnes, the antagonist, has a name that depicts someone who lives with the animals and has become one himself. Elias, his counterpart, has a biblical name that means "the LORD is my God." Even Barnes describes him as "a water walker," a reference to Jesus Christ. And Chris is short for "Christian" or "Christopher," a follower of Christ.

Now, Chris is torn between the two sergeants, Barnes and Elias, as is the platoon; half side with one, half with the other. Barnes has been wounded seven times and is seemingly invincible.

Chris wants to kill him for causing the death of Elias, but his friend Ra tells him, "Only Barnes can kill Barnes"—you have to become Barnes to kill him. In the end, Chris loses the battle with his moral self and does just that—and so did we.

We stopped trying to fight the enemy in a moral manner, as dictated in the Geneva Convention. Instead, we fought him on his terms. Many of us sank to the lowest common denominator, to the level of the godless Communists and to the amoral "Barnes" in our individual units.

In the end, it not only cost us the war, but our own humanity. That may be why the suicide rate for those of us who did manage to make it back is nearly double that of the non-veteran. Some of us couldn't live with what we saw over there; but I'm afraid more of us couldn't live with ourselves . . . for what we did over there.

Lesson #7: In war, it's not what happens to you that haunts you the most—it's what you allow yourself to do.

Chapter 12: Sgt. Edward Kaneshiro

We had our own Vietnam version of Audie Murphy on December 1st. His name was Sgt. Edward Kaneshiro. Here's part of the official record of his actions that day for which he received our nation's second highest decoration for valor, the Distinguished Service Cross:

Not knowing that the village was heavily fortified and garrisoned by North Vietnamese troops in vastly superior force, two squads of the platoon had deployed to its center, while Sergeant Kaneshiro and (his) squad scouted the more open terrain eastward. A fully bunkered and wholly concealed trench system ran the length of the village on the west side. From that source, machinegun and rifle fire suddenly came against the two squads at center, killing the platoon leader, the point man, wounding four others, then flattening and immobilizing the survivors. Sergeant Kaneshiro moved with his men to the sounds of the fire. Swiftly reading the situation, seeing the fire from the big trench had to be stopped if anyone was to survive, Sergeant Kaneshiro first deployed his men to cover, then crawled forward to attack it alone. He began by grenading from the parapet, while flattened, and his first round, entering the aperture of the bunker, silenced the machinegun and killed the gunner that had opened action. That done, with five grenades and his M-16 to sustain his assault, Sergeant Kaneshiro jumped into the trench to sweep its length, where it fronted the two pinned squads. Over the distance of about 35 meters, he worked the ditch alone, destroying one enemy group with M-16 fire and two others with grenade fires. By the end of his sweep, the able-bodied survivors of the two squads were again standing and preparing to move the dead and wounded. Sergeant Kaneshiro's assault enabled the orderly extrication and reorganization of the platoon which was the beginning of a larger action, and final success for the arms of the United States. Sergeant Kaneshiro's conspicuous gallantry and uncommon heroism under fire, at the cost of his life*, are in keeping with the highest traditions of the military and reflect great credit upon himself, his unit, and the United States Army.

Department of the Army, General Orders No. 46 (October 26, 1967). Home Town: Honolulu, Hawaii.

*Author's Note: This report mistakenly has Sgt. Kaneshiro dying on December 1, 1966. He was actually killed in another action on March 6, 1967. The Distinguished Service Cross was awarded for his actions on December 1, 1966, three months after he died on March 6, 1967.

The sergeants—like Kaneshiro, Cain, Samuel, and Haskett—really run a war. Officers see the Big Picture, make the plans, and give the orders, but the sergeants are tasked to find the way to make it happen. They make things work. They always have.
A lot of the 1st Cav officers were pilots. They were good, not because they were officers, but because they were good pilots. They led by example; you wanted to follow them. Our pilot/officers had another quality that set them apart from the rank and file: they were always there when we needed them, even when it came to flying in under fire to pick us up. And they didn't waste an hour or more debating the issue among themselves. Five minutes after they got the call, they were in the air, every time, no exceptions. They personified a literary double negative that was a big positive for us: they never said no.

Lesson #8: Good Leaders—whether Officers and Sergeants or Executives and Managers—lead by example, not by fear or intimidation. You follow them because you want to follow them.

Chapter 13: Hospital Life

"How are you doing this?" my dad asked on the other end of the overseas call.

"I'm calling from Japan," I replied.

"I know," he said. "But how?"

"I was shot," I said. "Didn't the Army notify you?" It had been two weeks.

My mom's voice joined his, "No." Their tone changed from elation to despair.

"I'm all right," I tried to reassure them. "I was shot through the right forearm in an ambush. There were 25 of us and 300 of the enemy."

Laughter and comments rose from doubters in my ward, "Yeah, sure, 300."

I looked at the mockers across the expanse of boney cots and dingy linoleum, wondering what their problem could be. Only later did I realize that their units weren't seeing that kind of action. They weren't the 1st Cav or the 1/9th or Recon.

This was the first chance I had to call home, the first wall phone I'd found in a ward. The previous week I'd spent in a small hospital in the Philippines. Half of the ward was ROKs: South Korean Army soldiers. They were all bed-ridden, some with missing legs. The G.I.s were in similar, though not as severe, straits. I was the only ambulatory (walking) patient on the floor, and since the lone black-and-white TV didn't have a remote, I was the designated dial twister.

The TV set was mounted on a wall next to the ceiling. Balanced on a rickety chair, I turned through the too few stations available. When boxing came up, so did cheers from the ROK contingency. The Americans protested.

"If you guys want to argue with the ROKs, be my guest," I said as I climbed back down to earth. All the Korean troops knew karate and were as hard as, well, rocks. Boxing won.

Approaching twilight, our plane landed in Japan and we boarded slate-gray military buses—not dissimilar to the egg-yellow ones we rode to high school 18 months earlier. As our casualty caravan snaked its way across the countryside, two young locals on one motorcycle darted dangerously around and in between our vehicles. We looked down at them as uppity Asians, their in-and-out antics flaunted their disrespect for our solemn column. They were still young and having fun; we weren't.

Some minutes later, after we thought they were long gone, our bus rounded a bend. The two young men lay sprawled on the side of the road, their bike embedded in a tree. Everyone on the bus erupted in laughter. They might have been seriously injured or even dead, but they looked like Wiley Coyote from some demented Road Runner cartoon. We kept on laughing. Even though they weren't Vietnamese, they were still subhuman in our book, not real people. Anyway, their dads had tried to kill our dads.

Another Trooper who had served in Europe before being reassigned to Vietnam, told me that the Germans would try the same thing with our armored convoys. And now and then, when they didn't quite make it, you'd see a VW flattened like its namesake "bug" on the Autobahn. They tried to kill our dads, too.

To the northeast of the fighting Vietnam brothers, Japan was a winter wonderland in December—cool, refreshing, safe. We needed our issued wool blankets at night. Regrettably, mine still said "us" on it, when there was only "me" under it.

There are asylums for the insane, criminally insane and otherwise, and then there are asylums for the lame and infirm. The latter are referred to as hospitals.

Now, the military can't admit to the former, so it combines the two into one institution, into an asylum for the criminally lame and emotionally infirm—because, let's face it, who in their right mind would purposely try to kill or maim another human being? The military minds, who for the most part walk to war, call these asylums simply Army Hospitals. Ours was called Camp Zama.

You may think a hospital is a hospital, but you'd be mistaken. Do the hospitals you frequent have food fights on the wards? Ours did. It served as both an outlet for our pent-up aggressions and a way to deplete the stockpiles of hard candy we'd received for Christmas. It began the way all wars do, for no particularly good or intelligently discernible reason, and then escalated until every man in the ward of a dozen beds was feverishly unloading at will. And of course, the already worst off got the worst of it. In our case, he was the helpless, hapless guy strapped to a tilt table at a 45-degree angle. He became everybody's favorite target. Hard candy, hard core.

Do your hospitals give you a job while you're recuperating? Army hospitals do. Mine was working in the Cast Department, evidently learning how to apply casts. But since they never needed me, I never did. Except for half an hour one day when I stocked a shelf with supplies, I went to the Rec Hall and played ping pong— every day, all day long, for a month and a half. I got pretty good, too, even with my bullet-branded arm.

The only time I wasn't playing ping pong was during physical therapy, learning to bend my fingers back and to squeeze a little rubber ball. Ping pong probably did more for me.

And how about Christmas day? Why, that was the one day I worked the hardest. From 6:00 am until 6:00 pm—that's 0600 to 1800 hours Army time—I fetched food for guys in wheelchairs or who otherwise couldn't manage for themselves. Then I policed up their tables, and swept and mopped the mess hall for breakfast, lunch, and dinner. I guess the Army forgot my Christmas present and wanted to make it up to me somehow.

You meet some interesting people in an Army hospital, more interesting than in a civilian facility. They're all a lot like you, with similar experiences and stories to tell.

Bob Steffans (r.) and me at Camp Zama, Japan.

One was Bob Steffans. He had been with the 1st Cav unit that came in to help us out on December 1st. He was shot and left for dead. Bob was all smiles when I knew him—all smiles, all the time. I guess that's the way you feel when you come back from the dead.

Another guy I met had a wound to his stomach. It kept closing over too soon and leaving a pocket inside, a cavity that became infected. So the doctors had to open him up all over again and start over. They'd done it twice before. The doctors had him swab it out every few hours to let the inside heal first. I watched him take a long cotton-tipped swab, dip it in hydrogen peroxide, and insert it through a small aperture on his stomach. He would move it around, cleaning the inside while trying to widen the small hole at the same time. It looked unreal, but it was his reality.

In combat, big guys can be a detriment; they stand out; they draw fire. For my money, they're only good for carrying heavy equipment, like machine guns. Give me a little guy any time. They make the best soldiers. They're a smaller target and harder to hit, plus they can kiss the dirt quicker under fire because they're closer to it. I know this for a fact—all the guys we fought were little guys.

(l to r): "Flo" Florez, Bethel "Smitty" Smith, Rowdy, and (front and center) Rudy Werley. Flo and Rudy were wounded friends we met at the hospital from other outfits.

But little guys are good soldiers for another, more fundamental reason. All their lives they've been looked down upon. Then an M-16—the great full-automatic equalizer—elevates them to everyone else's level and they like it. They take it up a notch or two from there. Soon, we're all looking up to them—just like 5' 6" Audie Murphy.

One little guy I met in the hospital must have taken it a notch too far; something snapped. Suddenly, he couldn't speak. I would eat meals with him and a few of his buddies. We would talk and laugh. He would listen and smile when something was funny. When I last saw him, they had just awarded him 100 percent disability. Naturally, they sent him home. Unnaturally, they sent me back.

A product of Southern California and a slave of Southern Vietnam, I always said I wanted to see snow again before I died. It seemed like a safe request considering the locales. Then, just before I left Japan, it snowed.

Chapter 14: Return to Nam

China Beach from ground level. I waded in the South China Sea, aid bags and all.

January 21, 1967
> *Sorry I haven't written before, but it's taken almost two weeks to go through channels back to Nam.*
>
> *For the time being (and possibly for the duration of my stay), I'm no longer in combat. I've been reassigned as a Hospital Corpsman to the 67th Evac Hospital near Qui Nhon on the coast. They say the profile derived from my wound (U2—permanent nerve damage and/or impairment) will end my days as a Combat Medic. We'll see.*
>
> *Write to my new address for the time being, but hold on to the old one; it's where I'll be headed eventually if my assignment requests come through. Because of moving, I haven't seen mail for 2-3 weeks now.*
>
> *If this is God's will, then I'll stay no matter what I try to do to stop it. If it's some ploy to tempt me with an easy time of it (good meals, wooden billets and cots, pretty nurses, no danger, hot showers, and easy working conditions), then I'll buck it every chance I get.*

The enclosed picture from the magazine (helicopter and troops) was accompanied by this story. The chopper is B Troop's, but the 32-man Recon force of the 9th Cav is C Troop.

I saw our guys on TV at the airport a few nights back (C Troop in Bong Son). Lookin' good.

Rode a 727 jet (three in the tail) back as far as the Philippines, but then was bumped off by VIPs (officers). Ended up in some old crate (C-130), camouflage and all, back to Nam.

Talked to the Chaplin here about going back to C Troop. The guys I left behind wounded when I was hit, screaming "Medic! Medic!" is finally (or again) getting on my nerves since I'm not going back. He'll talk to the C.O.

Write again soon.

Love, Brad

February 6

Well, this rear echelon duty (pouring concrete foundations for barracks, wrestling oil barrels and 110-lb sacks, plus shoveling gravel and sand, and digging trenches for 10-12 hours a day) has been good therapy for my muscle tone. I've got about 85 percent of my grip back.

I'm up to 157 lb now and tanned as well. Got a bad case of fungicidal infection of my left foot with lymph node inflammation in my hip; complications, but not too serious (just enough to allow me to rest up for a few days).

Finally going to get paid in a day or two (they'd lost my pay records back at 90th Replacement), so I can breathe again.

Dad, I'll check about that 10 percent interest Federal Serviceman's Bank Savings program, but from what I hear you can't get your money out until you leave the Service (the Army, not Vietnam)! I'm going to want part of my blood money long before that, so I may not go for it. (I don't trust anything having to do with the Government anymore anyway!)

No word on my orders back to C Troop, yet—hope to hear soon.

Linda has been writing. She's getting married in June. I'd like to make that wedding! Oh, well.

It looks as if I don't extend over here for another six months, that I'll be sent to Fort Hood, Texas, and an Armored Unit to come back over to Nam for another whole year! Hard decision to make.

I'm getting mail addressed to 67th Evac new address, but still none of my old address mail from C Troop.

Celebrated my 100th (Day) Anniversary in Vietnam on January 31.

Still haven't been assigned a Corpsman's job in the hospital (they're still waiting to see if I stay). I just do manual labor and help direct the Vietnamese workers. It's hard work, but satisfying.

I'm eating more now than I ever have and sleeping well (except for nightmares). The psychologist gave me pills to relax me and told me I was suffering from guilt complex and maladjustment to my new job.

Well, that's about it. (Your Son, the Nut).

All my love, Brad

February 13

Evidently my request was approved by its biggest stumbling block (55th Medical Consolidate Personnel) and I'll be leaving for C Troop any day now.

For the time being, I'm Assistant Armorer in charge of weapons disposition (mostly just for guard duty).

My fungicidal infection (left foot) wasn't clearing up as rapidly as it should, so the doctor here has me on a temporary profile. For two weeks, I can't wear boots (just low quarters).

The other night the USO had a show for us in one of the hangars at the airstrip. It was little old Nancy . . . what's her name? . . . Oh, yes, Sinatra. She sang "Sugar Town," "Boots," Frank's new one, "That's Life," "Summer Wine," etc. A group of long-haired draft-dodgers accompanied her, plus the boyfriend of "Kelly" on "The Bachelor Father" TV series—remember?

Ten days will mark the completion of my first four months over here. How 'bout that?

In these clippings: I think that's Bethel Smith (ex-tunnel rat in Japan with me, remember?). I know it's one of our guys for sure anyway.

I got paid $140, so I sent home my first batch of pictures. They'll be developed in Palo Alto, California, and mailed to you as prints.

I've been thinking about buying a 35mm camera (Kodapak film magazine type) to get my pictures made into slides for the projector. But since they'll be entirely of burning villages, wounds, and wounded I've treated, and dead VC, it might be in better taste not to. The shots from the helicopters would be worth it, but over there the camera is still likely to be ruined. I'll give it some thought.

No packages yet or mail to C Troop. Hope it's all right. Keep writing and praying for me.

Love, Brad

Qui Nhon, South Vietnam: the 67th Evac Hospital.

March 1 (Sunday)

Nothing much is happening here (67th Evac). My request to be transferred back to C Troop was approved by my C.O., but still must go through upper channels to be verified.

66

Tomorrow, I have an appointment with Mental Hygiene (Head Shrink) to talk over my problems (dreams, nervous stomach, and anxiety).

We've been pouring concrete for a new barracks here—lots of hard work and sun—but helping the muscle tone of both arms.

A chopper from C Troop landed here the other day and I got to talk to one of the guys. Seems I might have been awarded the Bronze Star for what I did for Sgt. Cain. Be nice if it was true. I'll mail it home if it is.

One of my good friends in C Troop (came over with me on the plane) is still going strong: Charles Roberts. Always said he'd give me the first enemy weapon he ever picked up for free. Heard he's got several now. If it's true, I'll have it gutted and send it home (AK-47, Chinese manufacture of a Russian design—look it up in my Gun Book).

Went to church today and it seemed to help.

No mail now for more than a month. Still being sent back and forth between Japan and C Troop, I imagine.

Saw "The Group" and "Walk, Don't Run." Very good. Also try "The Appaloosa" with Marlon Brando or "The Pad." "Not with My Wife You Don't"—Tony Curtis, Virna Lisi, George C. Scott, are very good, too.

Hey, Jody and Sharman, last night they showed "The Man Called Flintstone"—not bad.

Think about you all very much. Missing you all.

Love, Brad

March 5

Nothing much happening and it's almost time for me to hold patient mail call. Wanted to get these pictures back to you before we (Bill Vanover and I) took the afternoon mail out.

The doctors here say my hand functions are showing remarkable improvement (dexterity, strength, etc.) for the time elapsed. My nerves are restoring, too, though little by little. My muscle tone has suffered though, due to the loss of nerve impulses to certain areas of my right hand. Feels very bony and flimsy to the touch, but looks OK. I've learned to use my left hand as a substitute (like Grandpa).

All my love, Brad

March 14

I've finally made some time to write. Bill Vanover (the experienced end of our mail team) was transferred to Pleiku and I was left with both his mail call and the patient's mail call, too. It's kept me busy and tired.

I'm sorry I forgot to mail this Bank Card back before now.

I seem to be getting all your letters (by the numbers), so don't worry.

By the way, how much money do I have at home now?

Sgt. Kaneshiro (Silver Star winner and up for the Congressional Medal of Honor for his actions Dec. 1st with C Troop) was killed about a week back. Three of our guys were just here, so I got to talk to them. They were in the wards wounded, and painted a pretty grim picture. I've been out of the field so long I'm scared to go back. Seems my old First Sgt. and Senior Medical Officer were at 67th Evac looking for me and seeing the guys. They want me back since one of the new medics was wounded (only slightly through the ear) and they're short one. Time will tell.

Love Always, Brad

March 16

I just received 41 letters in a bundle (3-4 months old) from C Troop. My back mail was about 50 percent from the family. It took me 2¼ hours to read them all.

I expect the rest of my mail (just after I was wounded) plus my record player and raincoat will be along shortly.

Mom, I've got something that might explain Mrs. Forsyth's seemingly terse attitude about my mishap. I played a rather morbid joke on Dan (whatever your opinion of Dan, he is my best friend and I do expect you to respect our relationship and my choice of friends). I took the bloody, filthy remnants of the fatigue shirt I was wounded in, put it inside my personal effects bag, and then inside a Red Cross gift box, and along with a Christmas card, sent it to Dan. From what I gathered, Mrs. Forsyth either opened it or was with Dan when he opened it. I had sent a letter several days before (when I wrote you around December 2) to tell them what had happened; but just like the letter I wrote you, it never reached them.

I guess she must have been recovering from the shock when you phoned. Sorry, to say the least.

I got your birthday present today. I've been looking for art materials, but couldn't find anything that would suffice. During my stay in Japan, I did some sketching in an art class held by the Red Cross. Oddly enough, if anything, I've improved—possibly because it's more of a challenge now and I try harder. I'll do some sketches and send them home. Thanks again.

Got a letter from Tom Courser. He's on a destroyer now working around the Philippines (with the aircraft carrier Kitty Hawk). I'll write him when I get the time—also Rudy Werley (pictures) who I met in Japan.

I wrote Cheryl, too. Enough said.

Jody is going to make a first-class poet someday. What's Sharm going to be, a model or a cut-up?

That news clipping about my letter to Randy and the Editor's Note was as much as I would want printed. In good taste, too.

All for now.

Love, Brad

Post Script:

A Cub Scout wrote me—obviously part of some den project—not too long after I arrived in country. I responded and the letter was printed in our hometown "Duartean" newspaper. It was published on December 22, 1966:

The following letter was written to Randy Reagin from Brad Smith:

Dear Randy,

Thank you very much for your kind letter. It is greatly appreciated. Not much more than 10 years ago, I was a Cub Scout.

My mission in Vietnam is that of a Combat Medic with a Recon outfit. We conduct "Search and Destroy" actions against the Viet Cong, "Find and Fight."

I've made nine helicopter assault landings so far and have been fired on by "Charlie" (slang for Viet Cong) three different times. Today marks the end of my first month in Vietnam. We fly helicopters into the area and then walk up and down hills and jungles for eight more hours. That evening we are picked up by the helicopter and flown back to our base camp.

I know war may seem very exciting to you, but it is really a very bad thing. I pray you won't have to see it when you're my age. Be a good Scout, study hard, mind your parents, and most important of all, go to church.
Sincerely,
Brad Smith

Editors' Note: On December 1st, two weeks after the above letter was written, the 30-man patrol, including Brad, was ambushed by 300 Viet Cong. While administering first aid to a wounded soldier, Brad was wounded in the right arm by a Viet Cong bullet. He is credited with saving the soldier's life. After giving himself a shot of morphine, he and the other wounded were picked up by helicopter and flown to the hospital. He has had surgery for the repair of his arm and is improving very well, according to the latest report received by his parents. As far as we know, Brad is the first Duarte serviceman to be wounded in action and he will be awarded the Purple Heart.

March 27
My orders came through today redirecting me back to C Troop. We're only going out for 4-5 hours a day now during Operation Pershing, so it'll be easier on me all the way around (I'm putting in more hours [12-16] per day here at the Evac Hospital then I will be putting in per <u>week</u> with C Troop). No more pansy mail clerk either, I'll be working in my Mode Of Schooling (MOS) of 91B20.

Try to understand, it's what I really want. I want to come home alive and well, sure, but there are a lot of other guys who want to come home just as much as I do, but won't have the chance if I'm not there to help them. 1:30 am—I've got to get to sleep now—7:00 am Mail Call.

Brad

70

April 1

    Well, tomorrow I head for 15th Replacement at An Khe and C Troop in Bong Son. Write to the old address from now on:

        Sp/4 Brad Smith
        RA XX XXX XXX
        C Troop Medic
        HHT 1/9th Cav
        1st Air Cav Div Air Mob
        APO San Francisco 96490

    I've got to find some peace of mind and I think this is the answer. If it causes you mental anguish as to my safety and well-being, just remember to acknowledge God in all things—He protects those who believe in Him.

    If you can get some film for my camera (CX-127 Kodacolor) and some of those developing and mailing packs for prints, I'll get some good shots. I've sent two more rolls home of Qui Nhon and the South China Sea. Hope they turn out. They didn't pay me this month (March), so I'm a little short. Don't send any money though, I'll make out.

    Rumor has it that in another month or so, 1/9th is going to the Demilitarized Zone (DMZ) to do Air Mob Recon for the Marine Corps. May be assigned to the Corps. Good chance I might see Marshall. All for now.

                              Love, Brad

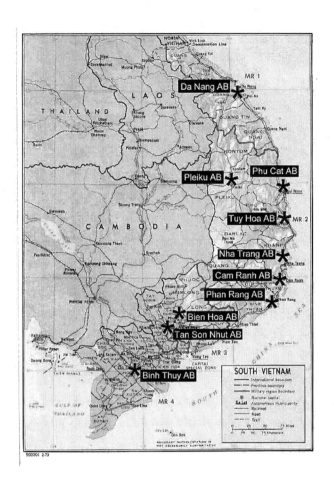

Chapter 15: The Monkey and the Medical Profile

I rejoined C Troop at its new forward base: *Two Bits*, a Vietnamese graveyard the Army had requisitioned and renovated. One last hurdle blocked my return to combat, a little parting gift from the Army doctors: a U-2 Medical Profile.

When doctors at Camp Zama first handed it to me in Japan, its implications were obvious and ominous. According to them, the permanent nerve impairment I suffered meant no strenuous exercise and no lifting more than five pounds with my right hand.

As an Armorer and then Mail Clerk at the 67th Evac, I favored my right arm over my left, letting my left arm do most of the work, especially when carrying weapons and mail bags.

Now, however, as I stood outside the Medical Tent to see the Flight Surgeon, I suspected what he would say:

'If you can't lift five pounds, how can you carry out a wounded man? No combat for you, Smith!'

I'd come too far to be turned back now. The 100-pound sacks of cement I wrestled with for days building barracks in Qui Nhon told me I could do the job. But what about the U-2 papers in my hand? They told a different story, the official medical story.

While I stood there praying about my dilemma, I watched the Troop mascot, a monkey, who was chained to the leg of a table outside the Medical Tent. The stupid thing was running around, half-crazy from the heat and the sun. Join the club.

Suddenly, the mad monkey reached up, grabbed the profile from my hand, and began tearing it up. I had my answer! I let it. I even handed it sheets it missed, while I laughed the whole time. When the hairy paper shredder had finished, I gathered the remnants and tossed them in the nearest 55-gallon trash drum. Then I walked into the Medical Tent, empty of hand and clear of conscience.

Inside, I met the real Troop mascot: a lifer sergeant and keeper of the medical supplies. He took an immediate disliking to me:

"You gave up a cushy job in Qui Nhon to come back to this?" he said. "Are you crazy?"

'Duh, we're all crazy here, Sarge,' I wanted to say. 'Didn't you get the memo?'

Over the next few weeks, his immediate dislike mellowed into a deep and genuine hatred.

"This is Specialist Smith with C Troop," he told the new Flight Surgeon. "He *volunteered* to come back to combat after being shot." He said it with real disgust, as if I was too stupid to live—which was yet to be determined—or he had just found a pile of me stuck to the bottom of his boot.

He questioned the supplies I wanted, too:

"You don't need that, Smith," he said, as I handled a box of single-edged razor blades.

"I do," I protested, "to cut off the clothing around a wound quicker."

He took the box from me.

"And you don't need these either," he said as he confiscated the petroleum-impregnated dressings.

"These I really do need, Sarge. They're the only thing that we've got to make a sucking chest wound air tight."

I won that one . . . and the first one, too, in the end: I just came back and took the razor blades and anything else I wanted when he wasn't around. What could they do to me if they caught me—send me back to combat? Shoot me? Been there, done that.

One of the first people I ran into back at C Troop was Charles Roberts. He looked genuinely glad to see me again.

"Doc," he said, smiling, "I got the guy who shot you. He was a sniper."

"Thanks, Charles," I said, and then smiled back at him. I knew from the low angle of entry, parallel to the ground, that the bullet that nearly took off my arm was from a bunker or spider hole. Snipers shoot you from trees. But I appreciated the sentiment anyway. Later, I found out that Sgt. Kaneshiro had most likely chalked up my NVA with a grenade.

That first night I was back, another lifer sergeant who didn't know me by sight dropped by my tent. I thought it was a friendly gesture on his part, until he started feeding me a steady diet of war stories—kind of a Welcome Wagon way of screwing with the mind of the new meat. I waited until he started telling about December 1st before I said anything,

"Was the Medic you had December 1st good?"

He looked at me funny, and then said, "Yeah, he was."

"That was me. I'm that Medic."

He said, "No."

That's when I held up my right forearm and brandished my stop-sign red scar. "What does this look like—a vaccination?!"

He looked at it, then at me, and then left without another word. I guess I'd spoiled his story hour.

The "vaccination" line was one of my favorites from some black-and-white 1930s Robert Mitchum movie rerun on TV I saw as a kid. There's another great line I've always wanted to use from a Mitchum film. He decks this loudmouth with one punch, and then as he's standing over him says, "You bounce real good." Of course, when Mitchum said it, you believed it. He had a mean way with words—especially after he'd just made you eat yours.

Picturesque, pipe-wielding peasant.

The Flight Surgeon, Capt. Schweitzer, seemed like a pretty decent guy, for an officer. You could tell he was a civilian doctor the

Army had kidnapped, air-brushed green, and shipped off to Nam too fast: he was still wet.

Morphine is G.I.-issued to Medics in handy little quarter-grain syrettes. It consists of one-tenth opium diluted in a nine-tenths saline solution: the ten percent solution. At least one Medic I know thought it was a solution for his personal woes. Meant for medical purposes only, he was self-administering it for recreational, in-country trips; kind of out-of-body R&Rs. One Trooper told me he'd shoot up on the trail with half a dose, and then offer the other half to anyone who wanted it.

The Flight Surgeon, alarmed at the disproportionate rise of use-versus-casualties, issued an edict requiring strict accounting of every syrette administered in the field.

"I used two syrettes today," I told the Tyranno-Sergeant Rex who was tasked to keep tabs on them. I helped myself to one of the lawn chairs inside the Medical Supply tent. I was hot and tired.

"OK, Smith, I'll need name, rank, and serial numbers of the wounded men."

"We've got a problem there, Sarge."

The sergeant narrowed his gaze. Maybe he was thinking he could throw an Article 15 at me or worse. I knew he didn't want to see me pulled from combat. He wanted to see me killed in combat. It would vindicate the superiority of his it's-safer-in-your-tent worldview. My death would make his day.

"They weren't G.I.s," I said. "They were Vietnamese."

He bolted out his lawn chair. "Gooks! You wasted morphine on Gooks!"

"No," I said, standing up to meet him head on, and hoping my voice didn't crack. "I treated a wounded farmer and a little girl. They were in a lot of pain."

The sergeant looked as if he couldn't wait for the Communists to do the job, he'd do it himself. Even though we were the same height, he outweighed me by 50 pounds. My 160 pounds out of Basic had withered away to 120 pounds in the heat, humidity, and general Hell of Vietnam. Plus, he was a full-grown man and I was still a boy, physically. Morally, I was his daddy . . . even his granddaddy.

Maybe because he thought I wasn't worth losing a stripe over or thought twice about messing with the senior Medic for "Certifiably Crazy"-Troop, the confrontation ended there.

As I walked away from the Med Supply tent, I considered returning with my M-16 and wasting him. After all, some of my nearest and dearest friends did it on a regular basis, and they never got in trouble. They killed guys they didn't even know, by the bushel basketful, just because their eyes slanted differently; and I hated this guy. He made my difficult life even more so. He had it coming. He was a disgrace to his rank.

Of course, it never happened. But one officer I knew did have his tent mysteriously burned down when he wasn't in it. And I'd heard of officers in other units being "fragged" with grenades by unknown—no doubt enlisted—assailants. Combat messes with your mind, big time . . . and so do Officers.

Combat messes with a lot of lives, too. About this time, the month-old Flight Surgeon, Capt. Schweitzer, decided to play Medic. He climbed aboard the wrong gunship on the wrong day. While it was making a run on an enemy bunker in the An Loa Valley, a round penetrated the aluminum instrument panel, passed between the pilot and co-pilot, and hit him square between the eyes.

I had twelve weeks of medical training; he had twelve years. He didn't do the math: I was expendable; he wasn't.

Lesson #9: Know your limitations. Know your place. Do your own job.

Lesson #10: Your greatest asset is knowing you're expendable.

Chapter 16: Cat Troop

Ace of Spades dropped by U.S. aircraft in Happy Valley, RVN. It supposedly was an omen of death to the VC. The VC, however, had collected an entire deck of them! Every man in our troop took one for a souvenir.

The Army's radio alphabet—Alpha = A, Bravo = B, Charlie = C, etc.—didn't work all that well in Vietnam. For one, the call letters for Viet Cong, VC, came out "Victor Charlie," which at the time, seemed like a joke. There was no way they could possibly win—unless we pulled out and handed over the war to the Communists. But by what stretch of the imagination could that ever happen? So, since we called them "Charlie" (and the NVA "Mr. Charles"), referring to ourselves as "Charlie" Troop never set well.

I thought we ought to be called "Cat" Troop. C Troop was catlike in a lot of ways.

Cats are hunters, some of the best in the world, and so were we. You don't bag half the kills of an entire division without being great hunters.

C Troop was cat quiet. The enemy never heard us coming. Each squad had a radioman and so did the Forward Artillery Observer (FO). We used them when we couldn't see each other, otherwise we relied on hand signals. If we talked at all it was in whispers, and not very often, and not very long—just a word here and there.

Both cats and C Troop were quick. Rowdy was on point one day when a VC came down the trail. The sniper had just fired on D Troop on Highway I and shot Doc Barkley through the knee. At 33, Barkley was old to be one of us. He had been a Medic in the Korean War. The VC must have been feeling pretty good about his prowess with an AK. But before he could even raise his weapon, Rowdy shot him stone cold dead—quick-draw style—like something out of Tombstone. Marshall Rowdy, rough and ready; he could have taught Doc Holliday a trick or two.

We were cat scary, too . . . as in Big Cat scary. In the chow tent alone one afternoon, with Doc Shore subbing for me, I heard helicopters landing nearby. A minute later, the hardest, meanest-looking men I'd ever seen were striding toward me as if they had just come back from Armageddon. Some sported Fu Manchu mustaches and all weighed in with serious attitude, armed to overflowing with M-16s, M-60s, M-79 grenade launchers, shotguns, and ammo belts across their chests.

Just for an instant, fear gripped me. Then I recognized them: They were C Troop! They were my guys!

"Man, you guys are one mean-looking bunch!" I told them. "For a second there, you even scared me." They just smiled, their expressions saying, 'Yeah, Doc, we know we're bad.'

And we were cat cool, too. Once, Cain and Haskett surprised half a dozen guerrillas sitting around eating their daily bowl of rice. It was back when McNamara still had us on a strict diet of ball, instead of stick, gunpowder. Cain squeezed the trigger, but nothing happened. Cool as a cat, he told Haskett, "Keep 'em covered while I clear my rifle."

When he finished and said, "OK," Haskett said, "Now you cover them while I clear *my* rifle."

Cat quiet, quick, scary, and cool—that was C Troop.

When your prey lives in tunnels, it pays to be a cat, too, and sometimes even a rat.

Bethel "Smitty" Smith was a Tunnel Rat. The first month I was in combat and still carried a .45 pistol, he would borrow it to search out tunnels we came across. With a flashlight in one hand and my rusty—I mean trusty—.45 in the other, he'd crawl in head first.

I often wondered how I'd ever be able to get to him—or get him out of there—if he was ever wounded. Things were scary enough topside. Pound for pound, Smitty had more guts than any of us.

Chapter 17: Sky Troopers

Wind surfing along the South China Sea.
Photo courtesy of Matthew Brennan, author of FLASHING SABER

The 1st Air Cav had its delights as well as its dangers. Chief among them was flying over the vista of Southeast Asia with all the grace and agility of the Ruby-Throated Hummingbird.

To refer to helicopters as aircraft, and equate them somehow with airplanes, is both a misconception and a misfortune. Helicopters are more akin to elevators, escalators, hot-air balloons, and Peter Pan. You rise in them as if by magic, effortlessly upwards, and then hover motionless above the world, while great waterfalls of air whirl down, around, and past you. Without doors, you clung to your life in the eye of a hurricane whose ripping winds rushed scant inches from your face.

Placid river and the lethal M-60.

Our slick (another slang term for helicopter) pilots liked to fly in formation, with the four lift choppers staggered and close enough so the rotor blades overlapped. Everybody on board thought it was the coolest thing ever, like flying with the Thunderbirds. Yeah, everybody on board just loved it . . . except me. I hated it. It scared me more than combat. It was a mass casualty situation waiting to happen. Hit an updraft or stray air pocket, and we were toast, molting out of the sky minus parachutes like crap from a goose. Fortunately, they did it once too often, and too close to Two Bits. A Cav General saw them, "Beautiful, Boys, beautiful job of flying. Don't let it happen again."

For my money, the view was the most exhilarating part of the flight. Why turn it into a carnival ride and ruin it with unnecessary danger? We were atop the Eagle's Lair. Without wings—and the war—to spoil the view, the spectacle below was breathtaking, postcard perfect. Like quilts, patchwork rice paddies covered the countryside. When they came to low-lying hills, these shelves of rice ascended in terraces like Jacob's Ladder, step upon step, each one a thousand years older than time.

Scattered by the hand of man, clumps of toadstool-gray thatched huts clustered along silver ribbons of light running to the South China Sea, which, in turn, lapped the shores of other lands more serene.

82

Then all this scenery was framed by layer upon layer of death-black jungle—denser even than the accumulated minds that stole our lives, our youth, and then brought us here . . . to view such beauty . . . from so far away.

Heavily armed teenagers with attitude are a must for fighting any war . . . and always have been.

Chapter 18: Matt and Marty

Matt and Marty were a pair. As the Forward Artillery Observer and his radio operator, they worked closely together, spending every day in the field side by side. They even shared a tent.

Yet, they were polar opposites. Matt Brennan was dark and handsome, even suave. John "Marty" Martin was scruffy, with side-kick looks. The first got the girls, the second didn't, but wanted them just the same.

Their philosophies of war were at opposite ends of the spectrum as well. Matt almost seemed to enjoy combat with a near-impish zeal. The difference between Matt and a Boy Scout is that the Boy Scout couldn't call in heavy artillery; Matt could and did—with telling effect.

Marty could not have cared less about the war. Nam was a major inconvenience for him, a detour on the road of life. He could have been a reoccurring character in "M.A.S.H."—right along with Clinger, but without the skirt.

Matt genuinely believed in what we were doing; Marty did not, with equal zeal. Matt's M-16 accounted for more than 17 enemy KIAs over three tours of Nam; in his one and only tour, Marty never fired his weapon.

Even though there was a lot of latitude in their makeup, I enjoyed them both. Matt was so perfect, right out of Central Casting for a 1950s war movie, that he was ready-made for a joke. I used to tell him, "You know, Matt, you're too good looking for your own good." He hated that.

Marty, on the other hand, was fun to make jokes with. He was sharp, cleaver, and intelligent, without being obnoxious about it. His family must have run in some major circles, too. Once he read a letter to me from his brother. It told how Allen Ginsberg, the renowned poet, had visited him—borrowed the brother's coat and then never returned it.

For me, both Matt and Marty were an island of calm and culture in a sea of insanity.

Matt and Marty taking a Boonies Break. Smoke 'em if you got 'em.

Chapter 19: Sgt. Willy Peter Haskett

When I could, I always walked with Sgt. Haskett's 2nd squad. So did Marty and Matt. I liked their company, but I also liked Haskett. Somehow, we felt safer with him around. In the movies, Morgan Freeman would be cast in his role.

Willy Peter Haskett was a soldier before most of the rest of us were even solid. He was 17 when he fought in World War II. He stayed in the Army following that war, fought in Korea, and then retired after 20-some years.

When Vietnam raised its Ho-ary head, Haskett reenlisted as a private. He was already a staff sergeant with C Troop when I joined them as a Private First Class (PFC)—and he had already been wounded four times. Three wounds was a ticket home, but Haskett opted to stay. He *was* home.

Willy Peter Haskett was a warrior. He was a pro who helped keep a lot of amateurs like me alive. The Officers just thought they ran the war; Non-Commissioned Officers (NCOs) like Haskett really did.

Sgt. Haskett and our barber (unknown to us at the time, a VC).

Chapter 20: Pop-up Target

Charlie and his more serious-minded cousin, Mr. Charles, had a nasty habit of purposely wounding the Pointman in the first seconds of a firefight. They waited for the Medic to run up to help. Then they *killed* the Medic . . . a really unfortunate scenario if you happened to *be* a Medic. This alone could account for our 94 percent casualty rate among Medics, more than double that of typical 1/9th Troopers. This targeting of medical personnel tended to affect morale, demoralizing the rest of the unit and rendering soldiers less brave than usual, once they realized there would be no one to come to their aid. It also demoralized quite a few Medics. In World War II, the Germans and Americans had an understanding. For the most part, they let each other's Medics do their job. Still, if you were a U.S. Medic in that war, you automatically received the Bronze Star Medal.

The only Medic I knew in our outfit who belonged on this elite "6 percent" list (neither KIA nor WIA) looked like the last terrier-mix in a dog pound. He knew he was going to get it. It was just a matter of when, where, and how badly. If you yelled "Boo!"—which no one did—he would have gone Airborne without a chute. "A deer in the headlights" also fits his description. His eyes almost spun around in their sockets when you talked to him.

Question: What's the last thing that goes through a bug's mind when it hits your windshield?

Answer: His butt!

This poor guy looked like he was nervously waiting for his butt to catch up to his mind. Mentally, he had already hit and splattered months ago.

Chapter 21: Doc Row

About this time, Doc Row returned from the hospital. We had never met. He had replaced me when I was shot. Then I had replaced him when he was shot.

During the firefight of March 6th—no December 1st, but bad enough—he had run up to help a wounded Trooper shot in the head. He managed to make it, but then the NVA who had shot the Trooper, shot off the top of Row's right ear. The impact knocked him down and covered his face with blood. He had enough "cat cool" to lie there and play dead when the NVA came over to confirm his kill.

Next, Sgt. Kaneshiro, who would be awarded the Distinguished Service Cross for December 1st, ran up to help them both. The same NVA shot him dead, again through the head. Everyone always thought Kaneshiro was some kind of invincible, more so than even Sgt. Haskett. Kaneshiro was like Sgt. Cain— they had already erected a cold marble statue of him, except it *was* no statue, it was him! His death changed us all. C Troop was never the same after that.

After Kaneshiro was killed, another Blue behind a neighboring tree tossed Row a grenade and told him to throw it at the NVA's position. The Doc overthrew his first try, so the Trooper gave him another. He got him on the second attempt.

Row's patient died sometime later in the hospital. His family was able to fly to Japan to see him first. I doubt if he even knew they were there.

Within five minutes after I met Doc Row, he blurted out, "I thought you were a stocky, black guy."

I took it as a compliment. Cool is hard to come by when you're skinny, white, and wear black-rimmed glasses.

I could sense he was nervous. "How do you feel about coming back?" I said.

"I'm really scared," he said. Why shouldn't he be? Some clown shot off the top of his ear and then killed everybody's hero Kaneshiro. Then the Doc had to play dead while that same goon stood over him wondering if he should waste another round on him or not. Who wouldn't be scared after that? Who wouldn't be *scarred* after that? I know I would.

Still, I knew he wouldn't have told anyone else about his fear—only a fellow Medic and only one who had been there and back, too. Medics weren't allowed to be afraid; we were only allowed to be nuts.

"OK," I said, "I think maybe I can help. They've had me over at D Troop for the last week. It's a milk run. You ride in a truck all day long and hardly see any action. I'll trade with you."

You'd think he was six years old again and it was Christmas morning, "You mean it? You'd do that?"

"Yeah, I really want to go back to C Troop," I said. "Deal?"

"You bet! Deal."

That felt good. I would be going back to C Troop permanently, which is what I wanted more than anything else, and I was helping out another Medic at the same time. My motives weren't entirely altruistic, but Row didn't seem to mind. Win-win.

We ran into a rear-area sergeant (his rear was an area all by itself!) outside the Medical Tent. He looked at Row like he was a rock star.

"Row, glad to have you back, Man. We just got the good news: You've been awarded the Silver Star!"

Chapter 22: Tent Life

My tent had been home to Sgt. Kaneshiro before his death on March 6, 1967.
I returned to C Troop a month later.

Living conditions in Nam are what you make of them. For enlisted men, tents ranged from your basic two-man pup tents, occupied by one pot-head who liked to fill it with smoke, to more elaborate digs. Four of the guys had pooled their talents and sweat to dig out a split-level home, partially below ground. It came complete with dugouts for their sleeping bags. They even collected the crates left over from 105mm shells to use as walls. You could stand up inside the 20-foot long mansion like a person. A lot of the rest of us hung out there on down days.

"Why are you guys always over here?" one of them said one day, letting his frustration show.

"Because your tent is the *coolest* tent," answered Charles.

My tent was nestled between two trees that helped support the five tent halves stretched over a foot-high wall of sandbags. It had belonged to Sgt. Kaneshiro. I moved in April 6—exactly one month after he died. Now I was sleeping in a dead man's tent in the middle of a graveyard.

Under a light camouflaged quilt and mosquito netting, I never slept so soundly. When I needed a breeze, I just pushed out one of the sandbags near my face. I took a calculated chance of catching shrapnel in the face if we were mortared, but the fresh air was worth the risk.

One afternoon during monsoon season, I fell asleep with my foot resting on one of the twin tent poles. I awoke only after my boot slipped off and landed in six inches of water! My tent was now a toilet.

In the pouring rain, I grabbed my entrenching tool and dug a canal around the perimeter of the tent. This diverted the rain running down the hill. Then I dug a deeper ditch to siphon off the water that had already pooled inside the tent.

While restocking at my friendly neighborhood Med Supply early one morning, I noticed half a dozen stretchers propped up in a corner. The T-Rex sergeant was AWOL.

"One of these would be good to have by my tent," I said, then searched for a viable reason, ". . . in case casualties are choppered to that side of the airstrip." The replacement Flight Surgeon agreed. He didn't really care. He left to look for ice for his beer—his idea of a medical emergency. He was no Capt. Schweitzer.

When I got back to my tent, I zipped my air mattress inside of my sleeping bag and put them both on top of the stretcher. Box springs!

Troopers Jones and Brown.

When I thought I needed to do laundry, I just tied the sleeves or pant legs of my fatigues together and strung them on the outside of my tent. Overnight, the monsoons did the rest.

We didn't wear socks or underwear. The rain often caught us in the jungle or outside a village and soaked us through. Then it would stop and the sun would dry us out. The canvas-sided jungle boots squeezed out the water through small, side ports. But if we wore socks, shorts, or undershirts, that second layer of material never dried out. Jungle rot resulted. Toes fell off . . . among other things.

"Doc," called the only guy in the Troop I didn't really like, "what do you make of this?"

We had a number of Southerners, black and white, and even though it was still the '60s, we were brothers. Olive drab and mud were the only colors we saw; sounds trite, but true. Pvt. Rednecker, though, would have been more at home in a pillow case with matching mattress cover.

He took off a boot and peeled off a sock. His foot and toes oozed with red sores and scales.

I looked at him with disgust, "You know what that is—jungle rot. You've been wearing socks just so you could get it and get out of the field." He looked back at me like I'd just run over his favorite coon dog. "But I won't be your ticket out of combat. I'll put you up on Article 15 charges first!"

I was the Troop Medic, not the Troop Den Mother, and I let a couple of the new guys know it in no uncertain terms. One of them had an older sister who was a nurse back home. She must have babied him his whole life.

I was sleeping in my tent one down day—dreaming about being somewhere else—when he woke me up.

"What have you got for this sunburn, Doc?"

"Your shirt!" I told him. "Put it back on. You're not at home and I'm not your sister. Don't ever wake me up again!"

He never did.

April 7

Yesterday, I went on my first patrol with C Troop. We made two LZs (landings by chopper)—one was to set up a perimeter around a downed chopper and the second was the standard "Search and Destroy" operation.

Pretty hot over here (Bong Son) right now: between 95-100 degrees and 80-90 percent humidity. We worked more yesterday than usual for this hot of a day. Before I got back, C Troop had been patrolling only 4-5 hours a day. Hope it resumes.

I took four salt pills and drank nearly three canteens of water. I'm carrying the M-16 now, 7 magazines (140 rounds) of ammo, and two aid bags—not to mention two canteens and a steel pot (helmet).

We've got quite a large force here with the Cav and elements of other divisions, too. The fighting has quieted down and many of the North Vietnam Army (NVA) soldiers our guys have encountered were living on green rice. The last real fighting encountered was over a month ago.

I received my record player and records the day I was going to leave 67th Evac. It plays great and the records (except for one I never heard before) were undamaged.

I expect the rain jacket before long. The summer monsoons should be here shortly. No mail yet from anyone, except for two "Duartean" papers from the Chamber of Commerce.

I'll write again, the day after tomorrow.

Love, Brad

Chapter 23: The Home Front

The greatest deterrent to doing any job in war is family and friends back home. At first, you miss them so much you can hardly stand it. Day after day the loneliness gnaws at your gut. Then, one day, it all changes.

The day it changed for me was the first day I stepped outside of my tent in the morning and didn't think, 'I wonder what my family and friends back home are doing?' Instead, I stepped outside and thought, 'I wonder what Marty is doing today?' That's when I realized my friends were here in Vietnam, and they were my family now.

As a Medic, viewing your buddies as family makes your job a lot easier. Who wouldn't die trying to save their family? When I looked out over the tents where they lived between the graves of Two Bits, I realized that was my job: to keep them that way, living—between the graves—not in them.

(l. to r.) Unknown soldier, Squirrel, and Weise on bunker duty.

"Hey, Doc," a Trooper called to me one morning, before we saddled up. "Hanoi Hannah just reported you killed, by name, on the radio!"

Now, Hanoi Hannah was our war's equivalent of Tokyo Rose—except she was no Rose. Her British accent sounded more like a British accident. And instead of gearing her programming for the grunts, she played high-brow music for the officers—which they didn't like either. We rarely listened to her.

The Army provided us with Christy Noel from the "Beach Party" movies with Frankie Avalon and Annette Funicello. Her voice was sultry and steamy, and who among us could forget how she looked on the big screen in a bikini? We seldom listened to her either. We couldn't; it hurt too much. She did more damage than a battalion of Hanoi Hannahs.

In answer to the Blue's announcement of my broadcasted death notice, I smiled and borrowed a line from Mark Twain, "The reports of my passing are greatly exaggerated." At least avid readers Matt and Marty would appreciate the reference.

That was twice now that I had made someone's KIA list. When Walker was shot through the eye and killed on December 1st, they thought it was me at first. I guess we looked something alike. The blood didn't help. What bothered me most was that one of those false—and hopefully not premature—reports might make it back to my family stateside.

I'm glad I didn't know about the 94 percent casualty stats for Medics at the time. Ignorance is bliss.

Chapter 24: War by Proxy

The 60 million fatalities caused by World War II, ending with new weapons capable of destroying an entire city at one time, left society war-shy. Atomic weapons mothered the Super Powers of the Cold War, and the Cold War itself. Paranoia reigned. Like two heavyweight champions, both with a KO punch in either fist, the U.S. and USSR were afraid to meet in the ring. They were both leery of that first blow.

Since squaring off in World War III would be tantamount to national suicide, they sought to fight by proxy. They went down the ranks of other countries, past the Cruiserweights, Light Heavies, Middleweights, even past the Welterweights, until they found a likely couple of Bantam or even Flyweight contenders to match up. Then the Super Powers taught them how to feint, counter, and slip punches; how to draw in their opponent or lie on the ropes and roll with the blows; how to sucker punch them or throw combinations; and how to block. They taught them where the vulnerable spots were—chin, nose, temples, solar plexus, kidneys, and rib cage.

Finally, they laced their own 12-ounce gloves and size 13 shoes on them—even if they were too big—rang the bell, and shoved them across the ring. If their man looked like he might be losing, the Heavyweight Champs might even come in for a round or two, like some demented tag-team match. In the end, the whole affair degenerated into some bizarre, convoluted spectacle—like Ultimate Fighters run amok.

The Korea brothers were the first to face off in 1950, North vs. South, with the U.S. and China joining the fray as the real main event. Russia armed North Korea and Red China, testing both its arsenal and its tactics against us. New weapons like the MiG-15, with one whole unit even piloted by Russians, went heads up with American F-86s. Flush from victory in Europe and the Pacific, we were under-trained and ill-prepared. We lost 36,000 troops. Even though the history books chalk it up to Northern aggression, in truth the Korean War was just as much a proving ground by proxy as the Spanish Civil War of the 1930s had been for Hitler and Blitzkrieg.

Vietnam was designed to bleed us dry, too, again by proxy: North vs. South vs. us—Russian weapons vs. U.S. arms. While we killed Vietnamese, Russian training and tactics killed us, 58,000 Americans this time. The only Ivans actually involved were some pilots of MiG-21s who shot down our Phantom jets by a margin of 2-to-1. Then there were the interrogators in the Motherland who grilled our captured pilots in Moscow, executed them, and buried the evidence.

Vietnam 1995: Meeting a MiG-21 pilot.
Not such a big man without your plane, are you?

By the time the USSR invaded Afghanistan in 1979, we had learned our expensive lesson, learned from the masters, and did them one better. This time, we were the ones who sent the weapons—AK-47s purchased from former Soviet-satellite countries and Stinger anti-aircraft missiles we built ourselves. Then Congressman Charlie Wilson lovingly placed them all in the hands of Mujahedeen guerrillas. After a decade-long struggle, 20,000 Russian names made the KIA list.

The final war by proxy took place in the region of the Persian Gulf in 1991. It would prove to be the main event, the fight of the decade. America's edge sliced up the competition. In Space, GPS targeting, coupled with stealth technology in the air, revolutionized bombing. We came at night, dropped one bomb per target, destroyed it, and then left unscathed. On the ground, U.S. M-1A1 tanks, clad in secret British-conceived armor, proved too much for the best Soviet Armed Fighting Vehicles (AFV) Saddam's oil money could buy. We lost four Abrams; they lost four thousand Russian tanks!

So, the score ended with an apparent 2-to-2 tie, except that the U.S. took the last two wars in such convincing fashion that a year after the 100-day Desert Storm War, the USSR folded like a busted poker player . . . not even able to bluff.

Generals Colin Powell and Norman Schwarzkopf were a big part of why we won. As Nam field officers decades before, they still had the bitter taste of being on the wrong end of a proxy war. They didn't much like it. So, in the desert where there was no jungle to hide in, they were in charge. They took those hard-learned lessons and used them to fight the war the way it should be fought—not solely relying on superior numbers and weapons, but winning tactics as well.

If they had been in charge in Vietnam, would we have won? Might we have headed north and captured Hanoi itself? We did have 550,000 troops over there at the height of the war, even though only some 50,000 were engaged in combat. The rest were support troops, a ratio of 11:1. Eleven-to-one . . . what a waste of resources.

Chapter 25: Body Count

Body count—that's what mattered most to the Brass and LBJ during my tour. When I arrived in country in October 1966, the 1st Cav was celebrating its 10,000th kill since arriving as a unit the year before.

I've seen jackpot figures on our kill ratio that soared as high as 158:1, supposedly at the peak of America's efforts. Sure, but that's only if you're smoking the "pot" in the jackpot!

Let's do the math for ourselves. On April 3, 1995—the 20th anniversary of the end of the Second Indochina War, a.k.a. the Vietnam War—Hanoi released its official casualty figures to *Agence France-Presse*, the oldest news agency in the world. It claimed that 1,100,000 Communist troops had been killed in action during the war. That averages about 140,000 KIA every year from 1965-1972. If we look at just the 58,000 U.S. troops killed (not counting other allies and ARVN troops), we averaged some 7,250 losses annually during that same time frame. That's a ratio of roughly 19:1.

On December 1st, our body count was 69 NVAs with a loss of 10 G.I.s (three from the 1/9th and seven from another Cav unit) for a ratio of 7:1—even though C Troop was ambushed and outnumbered by a dozen fold. When we surrounded an enemy-occupied village in the Crescent and bombarded it for 36 hours, the kill ratio amounted to 25:1. So from personal experience, I'd say that an overall ratio for the war of 19:1—in our favor—sounds plausible.

The VC/NVA were a lot better soldiers than those figures would seem to indicate. Air power—especially the 1st Cav gunships and their door gunners—made all the difference. Helicopters constituted the main event in Vietnam. They took us in and back out again, flew in ammo and supplies, and air evacuated wounded—which is why a G. I. had an unprecedented 99 percent chance of surviving his wounds.

Due to Huey Bs, Cs, and Ds, they called us "Sky Troopers" and we felt like something just short of the *Starship Troopers* of Sci-Fi genius Robert Heinlein. I would not have wanted to be anywhere near Nam without choppers. We might well have been left in the same fix as the French. Thank God for the Hughes Aircraft engineers and technicians who perfected the science and art of helicopter flight after the Korean War. And thank God for the skill and bravery of the pilots and crews who manned and maintained those marvelous machines!

Chapter 26: Turning Point

As I've said, the Hueys of 1/9th didn't carry doors and were mostly aluminum, so protection from small arms fire was about as substantial as a Coca Cola can. You sat four abreast, sardine style, with the tin lid already rolled up.

That's one analogy. Here's another: If Vietnam was a shooting gallery—which it was—we'd be the ducks. Except the ducks in a shooting gallery aren't shoulder to shoulder. They have a better chance. Even real ducks have it better. At least they have a Duck Season, a designated span of time when they can be hunted. We didn't. It was always "Open Season" on the 1/9th.

Of course, the pilot and co-pilot had armored plating on the bottom of their seats and along the sides, but that was it. They were officers and gentlemen, prized by the Army. They'd been hand-picked, screened, and trained. They represented Big Bucks, a significant expenditure and investment.

The rest of us could be readily replaced. We were expendable and we knew it. Everyone knew it.

While a new gunship and crew were flying shakedown along the coast, Charlie put 37 rounds through her and killed the door gunner. The Brass sent in C Troop to even the score. It's what we did and did well.

Like something out of D-Day, our choppers circled out over the ocean and back again—four, five, and then six times—like landing craft at Omaha Beach waiting our turn to hit the beach. While artillery pounded the enemy positions, we could hear the huge rounds rushing down on the target, like freight trains falling from the sky. We could see the shells impacting the woods below.

We felt what the soldiers and Marines must have felt two wars before, the exhilaration of the salt-water air tempered by the horror of what awaited us on the beach. This was an "E" ticket ride all the way, in a demented Disneyland where the passengers looked straight down, without seatbelts, during the tightest turns. I remembered my high school physics—G-forces and centrifugal force—and said again and again in my mind, 'I do believe. I do believe.'

Sitting on the far end, wedged against the engine wall, it was my job to feed the ammo belt for the M-60 machine gun. A hot shell casing landed on my forearm, on the site where I was shot on December 1st, and burnt me. Fear broke over balsa-wood breakwaters and flooded my conscious. Shot again? So soon? It was only my second mission back!

Even though I realized what had happened almost right way, the fear gate was awash and breached. The tide could not be turned.

We jumped off the skids onto the sand six feet below. Our feet never even got wet.

As we cautiously moved inland, running between and crouching behind trees, I released the safety on my death-black M-16. I loved the feel of its high-tech plastic and aluminum. It was new, sexy, and fit the contours of my hand like it had been tailored for me. Once again, I was fresh out of high school, patrolling the logging forests of Oregon with my AR-7 Explorer semi-auto survival rifle—also designed by Eugene Stoner—waiting for the next chipmunk to pop up.

The Blues were indiscriminately tossing grenades into bunkers. They blew half a dozen that way with no body count until the Lieutenant said, "Start checking them out first."

In Vietnamese, Sgt. Coung called into the pit of the next one. A woman and four children emerged. Ready to pull the trigger at the slightest provocation, I knew it could have been me who almost killed that young family. It was a wakeup call.

Back at my tent, I put my stunning black rifle down and picked up an unassuming little black book. As I thumbed through it, I came across a passage in Luke. To paraphrase, it said to me: 'When you were with Me, did you need a sword or money? Now, he who has money, let him buy a sword, too—he'll need it!'

I knew it was talking about Judas with his 30 pieces of silver, but I felt He was talking to me personally: 'An M-16 isn't a shield, it can't protect you. Only I can do that. Leave it behind and live.'

The next day, I confronted the tall Lieutenant about my decision not to carry a weapon. "I don't feel right about trying to save a life one time and taking a life another," I told him. Surprisingly, he said he understood.

That decision was a turning point for me. There would be another.

All too often these beautiful, personable people were collateral damage.

I've been avoiding this part of the narrative because of what comes next, the second turning point. My wife is the only other person I've ever told about it. The few minutes it took out of one afternoon of a single day have haunted me my whole life. Another man probably died because of what I did or what I didn't do.

The word was that C Troop was headed for a big action. It felt big; World War II big, as we ran from tree to tree for cover . . . and me without a weapon. Only my shades kept the others from seeing the fear in my eyes. After December 1st, I always wore them just for that reason. Windows to the soul are best left shut in a war.

Another mass casualty situation scared me the worst. Would I be able to reach everybody who really needed help, before the VC got me again? I was now carrying two aid bags and even a Claymore mine satchel filled with dressings. Would they be enough?

We caught three VC, a woman and two men, cold. They surrendered without firing a shot. Charlie had nothing on C Troop when it came to stealth. I watched them squatting on the forest floor like trapped animals. Even in defeat they were defiant. Their black silk VC uniforms, pajamas we called them, suited their moodiness. They looked at us with the purest of hatred.

One of our Long Range Recon Patrols (LRRP) of six men had just been overrun by the VC a few days before. The report that filtered back down to us was that they had been butchered. Another troop found them hanging upside down, their heads decapitated and jammed into their hollowed-out stomach cavities, and worse—but that's where my description ends.

I feared the Enemy, and because I did, I hated them. Fear always breeds hatred and Vietnam was a breeding ground for both.

"We've got a wounded one over here, Doc."

I walked over to the soldier who had called to me and stood next to him as we surveyed the man. His leg had been hit by shrapnel, rendering his whole left thigh into bloody hamburger.

"Why didn't you just kill him?" I coldly asked the soldier. He didn't reply. Reluctantly, I knelt next to the wounded enemy. Without exchanging words, his eyes and hands pleaded with me. For what: mercy, help, both?

My training surfaced through my fear and hatred just long enough to whisper, 'Tourniquet.' Fine, but I wouldn't waste one of my issued ones on him. I wouldn't even fashion one out of a cravat. Both were in short supply within the confines of my aid bags. I might really need them for our guys if things got worse.

I found one of the VC shirts nearby and a stout stick. I wrapped the shirt around his upper thigh above the wound, inserted the stick into the fabric, and began to twist. As I did, I thought, 'I wonder how tight I can make this tourniquet before this guy cries Uncle Sam?'

When he suddenly sat up and grimaced, I had my answer. I could feel myself smiling as I relaxed the makeshift tourniquet one turn, and secured it to the side of his leg.

I thought about administering morphine for the pain he had before I treated him and the pain I had just caused him, but thought again. 'You only have ten syrettes. Save them for your guys.'

Two troopers walked over and ended my dilemma, "We'll take him to the chopper, Doc."

I nodded, but inside I was thinking, 'Good. Now I don't have to waste one of my few large dressings on him.'

As I watched, each trooper grabbed one of his ankles and began to drag him to the helicopter. As his head bounced over obstacles along the way, I could hear them laugh; I could see them smiling at one another.

I might have been able to walk away from my moral and ethical failure, if it hadn't been for the interpreter, Tong. As I stood up, he was there, facing me.

"Do you treat everybody wounded same?" he asked. His tone and the look in his eyes weren't accusing. He just wanted to know—I suppose from one Christian to another—except today I feared we were one Christian short.

"I try to," I stammered, then weakly admitted, "I didn't do too good of a job this time."

The big action never happened. I returned to base that night with all my precious medical supplies intact. Someone told me the wounded VC never made it to the Evac hospital. He went into shock and died on the way.

I've regretted my actions or lack thereof my whole life. I didn't actually kill him, but I didn't do enough to try to help him, either. His blood is on my hands—you just can't see it because it's covered by the blood of Jesus Christ.

The turning point came when I determined never to treat another human being that way again, no matter what the circumstances or my fearful interpretation of them. My very next action would test the convictions of that commitment to the breaking point.

Half the troop had already entered the small valley and I had just noticed the huge pile of boulders ahead when,

"Crack! Crack! Crack!"

We hit the ground as one. I rolled behind the nearest tree, a palm of some sort. One round hit a branch above me; another went clean through the trunk. 'Great!' I thought. 'A banana tree.' I had cut a whole grove of them down with a borrowed machete one day, just for fun, and because the VC were eating the fruit. One swipe would cut down an 18"-diameter tree trunk and make you feel like Paul Bunyan. The inside of the trunk was like the inside of a banana.

We returned fire and the AK stopped. "I got him," someone yelled. "You're the closest," he told Pvt. Rednecker, "Check him out."

Rednecker climbed the rocks, looked down, and reported, "He's dead."

He wasn't. He was trying to wrap his chest wound. Two other guys disarmed him and pulled him out of his boulder fortress. They laid him out in a little clearing in front of the rocks.

One of our guys from Alabama had a drawing of a Confederate flag on his own helmet cover. A bullet had gone right through the middle of it, skidded around between the steel helmet and fiberglass liner, and exited out the back. I bandaged the superficial wound it left on his forehead. It also left him with a nervous, crazed look in his eyes.

When I finished with him, we joined the group surrounding the VC. No one was even pretending to help him. They were watching him die.

I stood with them for a moment, took a deep breath, and walked forward. "Alabama" was standing the closest.

"Here," I said, handing him a petroleum dressing. "Open this up for me." He refused. I couldn't much blame him. The VC had narrowly missed killing him. But then, he hadn't missed me by much either.

I struggled with the plastic wrapper, until someone else lent a hand. It was Matt. He tore; I treated.

Only an entry wound needed dressing; a bad sign for a chest wound. It meant the M-16 slug had ricocheted inside his chest, flattened out, and caused extensive trauma. And morphine is taboo for a chest or abdomen wound, it restricts breathing.

Two of the guys carried him out, not by the ankles this time, but using a hammock they found in the boulder caves. Since my gunshot wound, I was losing the grip in my right hand. That's why, when we weren't directly under fire, Matt would often help me tear open the field dressings.

I walked beside my patient as we ascended a steep trail slashed diagonally up a hillside. About halfway up, I noticed his eyes were no longer looking around.

"Wait a minute," I told his two stretcher bearers. I put my hand on his throat to check his carotid artery pulse, while I took a closer look at his eyes. They were dilated and his pulse was non-existent. I watched his chest for one final conformation: no movement.

"He's dead," I said without fanfare. "Dump him."

The pair tossed him to the downhill side of the trail. His body rolled once through the tall grass and stopped. We kept walking.

Even if his friends came back and found him, they'd just bury him in a shallow grave. And in Bong Son cemetery, a.k.a. LZ Two Bits, all he'd get would be a mound of dirt over his head—something we'd just sit on during a break.

Still, I was glad I had at least tried to save his life, even though Alabama never looked at me quite the same afterward. So what? You can't please everybody, and you can't win them all—the Vietnam War would prove that.

Chapter 27: Coping

In the midst of my fears, my daily doubts, my minute-to-minute mind games, I finally came to a personal realization: I'd rather die trying to do my job, than live the rest of my life knowing I was a coward. That simple creed helped me through. Once I owned it, once I made its premise my credo, fear no longer owned me.

Two Bits: Our home for the duration.
Photo courtesy of Matthew Brennan, author of BROKEN HELMET

"Cool" in Vietnam was not caring or, at least, pretending you didn't care. The hard-core guys all wore masks to that effect. I think it was a holdover from high school.

I was never considered cool in school. I wasn't a brain, either. I climbed rope in gymnastics, so my upper body and arms were strong for my weight, but I wasn't a jock; more like a joke.

I liked to make people laugh. My mom was the same way and my dad had a deadpan sense of humor. For me, growing up, it was a defensive mechanism. If you kept the football players laughing, they were less likely to be beating you up.

I clowned around a lot in Nam, between firefights. As a Medic, it helped inspire confidence. Only someone certifiably insane—with papers to prove it—would be a Medic. So, acting a little off—or a lot—was a plus.

One time, I conducted a mock interview. I held out the handle of my bayonet as a microphone and asked, "And what do you think about how this war is being run, Soldier?" A longshoreman would have blushed at the language that followed.

Another time, I was standing under a tree next to a dead VC whose leg had been blown completely off. Rowdy, now a sergeant, brought two of his "new meat" recruits over to show them what a dead man looked like. The VC's limb was lying next to the body. The recruits looked like someone had just run over their puppy. The moment begged for a tour guide:

"Listen up, Troops," I said. "Here we have the latest design innovation in Viet Cong. Notice that this particular model comes complete with detachable limbs, ideal for the close quarters of tunnel life."

My favorite prank, however, involved a smoke grenade. On occasion, we would "pop a smoke" to signal our position to the choppers overhead. Just to have something to occupy my hands one day, I picked up the pin lying on the ground from one of those grenades.

As I fiddled with it walking down the trail, I recognized that it was exactly the same type of pin attached to a green ring that was used on our hand grenades. Interesting.

An hour later, we stopped for a time while the guys on point checked something out up ahead. That's when I spotted Matt some 20 feet away across a small clearing. Now Matt amounted to a heavily-armed hallway monitor. He always carried at least four fragmentation grenades on his belt.

I nonchalantly walked up to him, careful to keep the grenade pin hidden in one hand. When I was right in front of him, I smiled, put both hands on the webbing of his pack belt, and jerked one hand away. Then I dangled the pin in front of his face.

An audible gasp escaped from his gaping mouth as his eyes opened wide in horror. His head dropped down to his array of lethal bomblets. I knew he was thinking he only had four seconds to live.

"It's left over from a smoke," I said. He'd prematurely aged enough.

As he raised his head again, his smile was a mix of two parts relief and one part "you really had me that time." I really did.

I never played that trick on anyone else, though it would have been a great ice-breaker for any new guys.

To cope, I even created a kind of superhero called—get ready for it—Medic Man. When I was younger, when I was cool in the summers and warm in the winters, and safe at nights, never hungry, never sick on my feet, never puking in my tent, or peeing in the jungle—because I still had a buffer zone called home and mom and dad—I used to take a pilgrimage once a week. I'd walk several miles to a little shop, fork over my dime, and buy the latest Batman comic. It was a big part of the mythology of my life at the time.

Now, in a comic-book war, where I couldn't turn to the last page to see how it turned out, that fantasy world returned. I imagined myself as a superhero, able to dodge bullets and jump out of harm's way. The twin aid bags belted about my hips became jet packs, lofting me over trees, rivers, hills, and away from danger, a la Commander Cody.

During cold Landing Zones (LZs), when our helicopter was still a hundred feet up, I would sometimes climb out onto the skids alone. With one hand holding onto the machine gun mount, and one foot on the skid, I would raise my other hand and leg out and away from the side of the chopper. Then, if I closed one eye to block out the chopper, and closed both ears to the shouts of, "Get back in here, you idiot!" it felt as if I was really flying, Superman-style.

Naturally, I knew I wasn't really Medic Man, or anything even close to him, but the fantasy helped. It was cool in the helicopter and particularly on the skids, the only time I was comfortable the whole day, which helped, too. In truth, I was still that kid trying to escape into another world. I wasn't crazy, just imaginative.

Of course, at least one crazy really did haunt our elite ranks: Grayson.

"How many Air Medals are you up to now, Doc?" he asked one day. I was the longest-lived Medic at the time, with more than 100 helicopter assaults, so it was a fair question.

"Four," I said, calculating the number for each award.

Grayson smiled. "I'd have 20," he said, "if they counted that high."

"Twenty?! That's 500 missions!"

He kept smiling, big and wide, and not quite all there, like the Cheshire Cat.

Not too long afterward, I saw him cutting off the ears of a dead VC. "Souvenirs," he said, smiling again. He started taking fingers, too, I heard, until the Brass stopped him.

Grayson wasn't born bad. He was the towheaded kid across the street who walked your sister to school every day freshman year. He loved baseball, but couldn't catch a grapefruit. He got mostly Bs and some Cs.

Then the Army gave him something addictive to smoke: the M-16. They put it on full auto, pointed him toward Southeast Asia, and just left him there.

No, Grayson wasn't a bad sort; he'd just been over there too long and gone out too many times . . . 500 too many.

"Why do some of the guys wear the leather shells to their gloves in their helmet bands?" I asked Matt one day on the trail. "Hunter has one on each side. He looks like Mickey Mouse."

Matt replied, "Each glove stands for five kills."

"Oh," I said, and then shut up. I'd saved five lives in five months, maybe I should have stuck a rubber hospital glove in my helmet band!

The real killers in C Troop, however, weren't on the ground; they were in the air: the gunship pilots and door gunners of 1/9th. Quite a few of the door gunners belonged to the "100 Club"—that's 100 confirmed kills. That's how the 1/9th tallied up half the total kills of the entire division. They didn't make enough gloves or room in a helmet band for them.

I wondered if there'd be room in the real "civilized" world for them if and when they ever returned. I remembered seeing the black-and-white movie, "The Man in the Gray Flannel Suit." It dealt with a World War II combat vet who had returned to the corporate world, but he was still haunted by the memories of what he'd done in the war. Soon, my buddies would be living it . . . and so would I.

Bringing up the rear with my M-16 during the two weeks I carried it.
Photo courtesy of Sgt. Tong, ARVN Interpreter.

April 13

Pretty active yesterday. C troop and I made three copter landings (one of them "hot"—firing our weapons).

We initiated the day by landing in a rice paddy where about 20 or more so-called peasant farmers were hoeing a field. Since I've been in country, I've never seen more than <u>two</u> farmers in one paddy at any one time—neither had any of the other guys! We weeded out about five of them who were obviously VC—pack-strap marks on their shoulders, excessively blistered hands (from not working much and then working all of a sudden), or extremely smooth hands. One joker had a fatigue uniform on; knew he was in the army, but didn't know which one!

Next LZ was a field where two Joes were walking. Both had at one time been VC, were captured, or surrendered, rehabilitated, and now supposedly were "friendlies." We took them in anyway . . . "friendly like."

Then at about 3:30, we landed on a rocky mountain top and found several VC caves; stores of food, tomatoes, rice, etc.; and an

IV bottle filled with drinking water. We searched the rocks and streams for about two hours and then took off.

These three LZs were my 17th, 18th, and 19th—just 6 more and I'll have the Air Medal for my collection.

Dad, the interpreter (Sgt. Coung, who I bunk with) gave me this dried fish. Heat and eat (I ate two and lived).

Love, Brad

Chapter 28: Our Allies

My tent mate, Sgt. Coung, of the Army of the Republic of Vietnam (ARVN)—not to be confused with the Army of the People's Republic of Vietnam, a.k.a. the Enemy—asked me a question one night:

"Do you know Starwets?"

Now, when you bunk with a Vietnamese interpreter, there's no one to translate his English into your English, so you have to work at it. Except it was late, past 9:00 pm, the day had been hot, then wet, then hot again, but boring, wonderfully, peacefully boring. No contact. I was tired beyond belief, but the two of us never talked much. Marty and Matt talked into the "wee" hours, past 10:00. So I made an extra effort to accommodate the interpreter's question, whatever it was.

"Starwets? . . . Starwets. . . . Starlets!" I repeated. "Hollywood Starlets?"

His eyes filled the frames of his glasses to overflowing. "Yes, Howeewood Starwets!"

"I don't know any myself," I said, then saw his eyes begin to pinpoint, "but I've heard about them. I know about them."

"I read about them," Coung said. "I like to go to Howeewood, to America, and meet one."

'I just bet you would, Tiger,' I thought. 'You're dumpy, short, wear glasses, and as poor as the rat that invades our tent every night. Yeah, you'd be quite a catch for any wannabe Howeewood Starwet.'

"Sure," I said. "Maybe you will someday—after the war."

We had just blown out our only candle, the one I used to cook the "fish jerky" Coung gave me, when the nightly Rat Express arrived. At least, we thought it was a rat. Even though it played the cans in our stolen C-ration box like Ringo Starr, we never actually saw it.

Coung tried, though, and herein lies the problem. He'd grab his World War II-era M-1 Carbine and his G.I.-issue flashlight, and would sit up looking for it. Since our whole digs measured a scant 8' X 6' and maybe 4' high, I reasoned I was well within his field of fire, if not his kill zone all together. And when your roomie likes to be called "Cong"—and you just found out the base barber who

116

always cut your hair was a VC—you look for somewhere else to sleep.

So I grabbed my camouflaged quilt, told Coung he was crazy, and left the premises. Since I did this virtually every night when it wasn't raining, I knew right where to go. Thirty yards from our tent, between two trees, hung a double-wide, plastic, captured VC hammock: the best war souvenir the Blues ever swiped.

After gingerly positioning my 120-pound frame to actually lie in the hammock and not next to it in a painful heap, I covered myself with the downy quilt—blending into the scenery of course—and enjoyed the starry night. In short order, the cool breeze rocked me to sleep.

Sometime around 1:00 or 2:00 in the morning, a sniper would open up. His random, unaimed shots in the dark served as my wake-up call. I'd bundle up my blanket and return to our tent, where Coung had been sleeping without the rat for several hours. This scenario repeated itself night after night, until the President of the Republic of Vietnam—not to be confused with Ho Chi Minh—intervened.

President Thieu came on the radio and announced that he was extending the tours of duty of all ARVN military personnel by ten years. Ten years! Sgt. Coung went AWOL—as in deserting, ain't never comin' back—the same day. We—as in the rat and me—never saw him again. I like to think he made it to Hollywood—as a talent agent.

Nobody blamed him; a decade more of the war was incomprehensible. Ten days longer would have been too long for most of us.

There was also the little matter of a bounty on the heads of interpreters. A VC soldier stood to collect $100 for every interpreter he or she killed or captured. That amounted to at least a year's pay. Green Berets earned them $50. Medics garnered $25. I've always said that was the one time in my life I knew my true worth.

(l. to r.) Weise, Marty, and Tong.

Sgt. Coung's replacement was taller, slimmer, and a lot better looking. He seemed different somehow, too, like the ten-year extension and even the war itself weren't the end of the world for him.

"You no carry gun?" Sgt. Tong asked me one day on patrol.

"No," I said, hesitated, and then explained, "I'm a Christian." I wondered how a Buddhist would take that.

Tong smiled and said, "I too Christian." Then he put his hand on the grips of his .45 sidearm. "I carry this in case VC capture me." He raised his extended index finger up to the side of his temple. I nodded that I understood. A captured ARVN interpreter would not die easily or soon at the hands of the Viet Cong—especially if they found out he was a Christian.

One of our few viable allies in Vietnam, the Republic of South Korea or "ROK" troops, as we referred to them out of respect, were infamous for their brutality against the VC. When I was in the hospital, I had the opportunity to sit with some ROK officers during breakfast. They spoke English.

I asked the ranking officer, "When you go through a village, you kill everyone and everything—men, women, children, even animals. Why?"

"If you had the Communists overrunning your country, like we did, you would too."

April 15

Teamed up with a platoon of 1/7th Cav yesterday to brave the hell of An Loa Valley.

We made my 20th LZ on the top of a high mountain and began to work our way down. 1/7th Cav went ahead of us on point. They received sniper fire which wounded their Lt. and one machine gunner. Their medic took care of it.

A Long Term Recon Patrol (LTRP) outfit (6 men) had been overrun and wiped out with the loss of all their equipment (special night vision sniper scopes, M-16s, and radios). That's why we were sent into the area.

We didn't want to follow in the footsteps of 1/7th Cav, so we diverted our course. We got orders to leave the area, were picked up by choppers on a hastily cleared Pickup Zone (PZ) and let artillery and air strikes (F-105s with mini-guns and rockets) reduce the mountains, jungle cover, caves, and rocks to burned-out rubble. Made Base Camp about 6:30 that evening.

Got the pictures of the LA airport, sisters, and family. Thanks. I hope my pictures get to you soon.

Love, Brad

(l. to r.) Unknown Radio Operator, Sgt. Lonnie Samuel, and Aussie Soldier.

Another one of our hard-core allies was Australia. They were tough, good soldiers. We patrolled with some Aussie troops one mission. They wore these great hats, turned up on one side. They looked so cool. My helmet felt like a toaster continually set for four slices on the top of my head.

Years later, I worked with a young Australian lady named Sue. One day she confided in me, "You know, Brad, Australian men think all American men are wimps."

"Well," I replied, without a hitch, "compared to Australian men, we are."

Chapter 29: Rumors of War

April 17

Just got the word last night that C Troop is moving up to Chu Lai (The USMC base where Marshall is stationed) come the 20th of April. We'll be the only 1st Cav outfit up there at all, performing Recon missions for the Airborne, Marine Corps, and the 11th Armored Cav.

I'll look up Marshall (send me his address and tell him I'll be up there, so he can come see me, if I can't get over to see him). Should be interesting when I see him; the only Air Cav Trooper (except 31 others of C Troop) he's ever seen.

We wouldn't be going up to help out the Marines if we weren't the <u>best</u>.

I'm not carrying my M-16 rifle anymore—can't abide by killing even if it's so-called self-defense. I carry bandoliers of ammo for the other guys though and if I ever <u>need</u> *a weapon that bad, I'll pick up one from one of my indisposed patients.*

That's about it, then. Looks like busy times ahead.

Love, Brad

April 18

On "stand by" today with no intended mission.

Trying to square away all my gear for the big move up North to Chu Lai. I know God is with me every step of the way. His Word is my only weapon and His salvation my shield. "Though I walk through the valley of the shadow of death, I fear no evil, for God is with me."

So, Marshall made Sgt.—there'll be no living with him now!

These are my 44th Medical Group Patches I wore when I was connected with 67th Evac Hospital. Thought you might like to have them for the Scrap Book.

Dan just recently participated in the Spring Mobilization to End the War in Vietnam (March on San Francisco, April 15).

In answer to your questions on the merits of the war, I truthfully can find few. Lyndon seems to take the view that the needless destruction of young lives when concrete goals are unattainable is good for the economy. Government contracts for war implements are flowing like blood.

About it for now.

Love, Brad

Chapter 30: The USMC

In Vietnam, the tacticians for the Marine Corps were mired in the memories of past glories. They longed to storm beaches, but there were no Tarawas. They dreamed of taking mountains, but there were no Suribachies. They wanted to liberate islands, but there were no Iwo Jimas.

But they tried anyway, and died.

In Chu Lai, the Marines couldn't even take a step outside the base perimeter without drawing fire. It was so bad, in fact, plans called for C Troop to move up north to recon for the Corps. I entertained the thought of fighting side by side with them after being turned down as an enlistee—but it never happened—at least not while I was there.

The Marines had the spirit and the guts; but besides their tactics being 30 years behind the times and terrain, so was their equipment. Where we had Hueys, they had Korean War-vintage choppers—cumbersome, slow, and twice the target—if they had helicopters at all. When I worked at Mission Aviation Fellowship (MAF), long after my war, Ron, an ex-Marine helicopter pilot worked across the street. We had an entertaining inter-service rivalry. He had flown CH-46 medium-lift choppers, already considered past their prime in Nam. His assistant at their office in the MAF hangar, Scott, was in the Marine Reserves when Operation Desert Storm blew in. I remember as they waited to see if Scott would be called up—to pilot the same antiquated chopper in the Gulf War!

Of even more importance, where the Army had state-of-the-art M-16s, the Marines initially carried the M-14.

Now, an infantryman's rifle is supposed to be his best and closest friend. The M-1 Garand was every bit of both for our dads in World War II. So following that war, Ordinance decided to take the basic M-1 and turn it full-automatic. Simple enough, except it took them 15 years—and $20 million—to "perfect" it!

In 1966, the Army was still using the M-14 in Basic, even as it transitioned to the superior M-16 in the field. We were issued the M-14 with the selector switch permanently locked on semi-automatic. We never, ever fired them on full-auto. That's because by the second round, maybe the third, the M-14 would be shooting several feet above its intended target. It was so erratic that it endangered low-flying birds!

The M-14, still all steel and wood, also weighed a full five pounds more than the aluminum and plastic M-16. That meant more strain on the soldier's hands, arms, shoulders, and back—thus more fatigue—and less ammo he could carry. And its bulk and ungainly length made it that much more difficult to move at a moment's notice, especially in thick foliage.

Old tech, old tool, old school—in essence the M-14 was an M-1 with a bad facelift, a botched job that even in the dim light of a jungle trail showed its age. Historically, the Corps has always been the Cinderella of the Armed Forces—the last in line for everything. But Cinderella needs a Prince Charming, and the M-14 was no Prince . . . not even a best friend. Marines loved it anyway, but thus is the nature of love: often blind and long-suffering.

The lack of first-rate equipment wasn't the Marines fault. The Navy considered them a subsidiary; the Army envied their image; the Air Force longed to fly their close air support. The Corps deserved better. They've earned it.

If I had realized my boyhood dream and been accepted by the Marine Corps, I would have died in Vietnam. For sure. No doubt.

April 21

Some good news: We aren't moving to Chu Lai, at least not yet. Looks like we'll just work this area for a while longer.

We just got our new Flight Surgeon, Capt. Green. Too early to tell what he's like.

The enclosed ace of spades was one we found in a VC hut. He had a whole deck of them that our planes have been dropping. They are a superstitious symbol to the VC—meaning their death.

I ate in a VC "hooch" (hut) yesterday before we burnt it down. We were coming into a "hot" LZ (helicopters had sighted a VC mortar platoon coming to pay us a visit). Bethel Smith was on the machine gun and I was the assistant gunner feeding him the ammo belt. We had just about expended all our ammo and were setting down to land when Smitty put his hand on the hot barrel to secure it. He got a second degree burn from it. I treated it. He's all right now.

Enclosed is a picture mostly of me, "Marty" John Martin, and Charles Roberts.

About it.

Love, Brad

April 23

I've had a bad cold the last few days (102 temp at its worse and bad sore throat). Under 101 degrees yesterday and down to normal and possibly below today. That might mean it's malaria, but I doubt it.

Didn't go out yesterday. Doc Shore, my alternate, took my place.

I'm taking my temperature now to make sure.

Got 1.5 million units of Penicillin, injection and tablet form, and aspirin. Being a Medic comes in pretty handy in a time like this.

Thought my pictures turned out pretty good.

Able to eat a little now. I'll build up my strength and maybe go out tomorrow.

We took a "suspect" VC the other day. I found shrapnel wounds (old and healed) all up and down his left leg. He tried to tell us it happened when he was sitting on two chairs and fell and pinched his leg between them (ha, ha).

Temperature at 900 hours: 98.5 degrees.

About all.

Love, Brad

Chapter 31: Casualties of War

Basically, there is one of two ways to die in a war: brave or dumb. Dying brave is preferable, though dying dumb is more common. Either way, you're dead . . . basically.

I almost died dumb a lot more times than I almost died brave: almost skewering myself on a cross-bow booby trap, almost jumping into a pit of vipers, almost falling out of a helicopter . . . you get the picture. The operative word here is "almost"; it makes all the difference.

Unfortunately, however, there were a few of us too dumb for combat, and therefore, bordering on too dumb to live. PFC Peabody was one of these dangerously incompetent combatants assigned to our elite unit. By my estimation, there was maybe one other who slipped through the filters while I was there. Here's a couple of good examples of why he shouldn't have been in Nam:

We were sitting around at Two Bits reading our mail, when Peabody looked up and said, "My wife's pregnant! We're going to have a baby!"

Now Peabody had been with C Troop for a quite a while. "How long have you been in Nam?" one of the lifers asked him.

"Eleven months, Sarge. I'm short."

"Then it's not your baby."

"It's not? How do you know?"

"Because, PFC Pea Brain, babies only take nine months to be born."

Peabody reupped for a second tour of combat with C Troop. "I must be doing something right, to survive this long." This got him home early from his first tour, just in time to divorce his wife.

Then there was the last day he was in the field. We were walking along a winding trail, strewn with booby traps. It was flat with doglegs to the left and right, bordered by sand pits. It reminded me of some bizarre miniature golf course for sadists and masochists. Some of the booby traps were designed, like Bouncing Bettys, to pop up and explode waist-high—ruining your day. A G.I. golfer could lose more than one ball in a trap like that.

Our resident pros, the lifer sergeants, were going ahead of us, spotting booby traps and marking them. One they had found was a particularly nasty and cleaver devise. It consisted of a poorly camouflaged punji stake pit discretely connected to an explosive charge. If you found the pit and tried to dislodge the stakes, it triggered the explosives.

I walked around it with great care and then continued around the next bend. Not thirty second later, a horrific explosion sent us diving for the dirt!

Once down from reflex reaction, I was up and running back toward the reverberating sound. One body lie sprawled on the ground: Peabody. After Sgt. Haskett had explained to him why we all had to go around the punji pit, Peabody had kicked at the stakes anyway.

Maybe the rain had soaked the trap enough to render it ineffective. Maybe a Peabody counterpart with the VC had failed to fill the tube with fragmentation, so only the concussion hit him. Or maybe there really is a special Providence protecting idiots. Peabody wasn't dead or dying or even wounded. No blood. Nothing broken. Just temporarily deaf and as limp as pasta primavera.

He and the Troop had dodged death that time. The problem is that these dead heads not only get themselves killed, but good men with them.

Cooler heads took dead head out of combat after that. The last time I saw him, Peabody was working in the Mess tent. Marty was in line in front of me trying to get Peabody to stir the eggs to scramble them, while he just chopped at them with a spatula.

I'm sorry now we told him about his wife's unfaithfulness. Their marriage, like their happiness, might have been an illusion, but it was all he had—and in Nam, even illusions are better than reality.

May 3

 This makes the fourth day I've gone out in a row. Doc Shore, my alternate, is in An Khe for a few days I let him have off. He went out for me while I was sick, so I thought it was only fair.

 Our gunships and artillery killed two VC yesterday. We were dropped into the area to find their bodies. One was in a rice paddy shot through the head and the other was in a hut.

 VC terrorists killed an old woman who refused to give them rice, and we had to dig up her grave to get some pictures. General Westmoreland is pushing war atrocities perpetrated by the Viet Cong—for propaganda.

 The VC have been forced to retaliate upon the villagers for their lack of support. The VC's whole tactical structure is failing.

 Finally got my rain jacket and rain pants in the mail. They look great and I'll take some pictures with them on. Also got the records (45s): Beatles, Sinatra, etc. Thanks.

 We ran into some exploding booby traps the other day, but the guys spotted them before they were tripped and disarmed them. One was an Air Force bomblet and the other one was one of our own grenades with the pin secured to a trip wire.

 About it then. If I'm off tomorrow, I'll write again.

Love, Brad

Chapter 32: Bloodsuckers

"Every puddle has its leech." If this isn't an old Vietnamese proverb, it should be. During the monsoons, the leeches were out in force, drawing more blood than the enemy. In fact, you were smart to step over puddles when you could to avoid having one or more of them crawl up your boot. That's why we always "bloused" our pant legs tightly into our boots, to keep leeches from feasting on our legs.

Even so, they smelled or somehow sensed us coming. I stepped over a puddle once and happened to look down. As my foot cleared it, three leeches raised up, like dogs begging for a bone. They balanced on their tails trying to reach me. It still gives me the willies.

When you're on your feet 10-14 hours a day, especially when you're climbing up and down steep terrain in 100-plus degree heat, through dense jungle foliage, you ache to sit down—anywhere and anytime. Whenever I could, I'd doff my helmet and sit on it. One time, I failed to check it close enough before putting it back on.

Fifteen minutes later, I was sweating bad enough to take it off again to wipe my face. As my hand crossed my forehead, my fingers ran across a large, fleshy lump. 'Is that a zit?' I thought. 'No, it couldn't be; it's too big.' Then I knew!

"Pssst!" I called to the trooper in front of me. He turned and then looked at me like I was something out of a low-budget horror movie. He motioned to two other guys to help.

The leech was as thick as my thumb by now—after his Thanksgiving meal of me, Turkey Trooper. He was probably thinking about loosening his itty, bitty belt and watching the Bloodsuckers Super Bowl on his itty, bitty boob tube.

Now, you can't pluck off or cut off a leech from the site of the wound. If you do, it leaves tiny teeth and other mouth parts in the opening that can easily become infected. Also, the leech injects a blood thinner into the wound, so you bleed even faster. No, you have to encourage a leech to drop off willingly, of its own accord. Whispering sweet nothings in its ear doesn't work. No ears.

My distinguished team of medical experts first tried squirting me repeatedly in the face with insect repellent. When that failed, the one who was smoking applied his cigarette butt to the leech's big, blood-filled butt. Fortunately, this worked and the sucker dropped off—thankfully before the inflammable repellent had a chance to ignite and fry my face.

With the leech gone—and dead after I squashed it with the heel of my boot—the now open floodgate of my wound bled freely all down the side of my face and across my eyes. I was now a Technicolor version of "Dracula." The Troop continued toward the PZ with little notice of me or my personal medical emergency.

"Do you think we could stop long enough so I can put a dressing on this?" I pleaded.

Evidently, not. Must have been some provision of the Geneva Convention I missed that forbids such self-treatment on the go. It's not like I had saved any of them or anything like that. After all, I was only the Medic. I ended up treating myself in my tent back at Two Bits.

Besides the stray leech—not counting gunshot, shrapnel, and booby trap wounds—malaria was one of our biggest threats. Mosquitoes fed on us more than leeches, so we had to dose up against malaria. We took small white pills every day supplemented by a large "horse pill" every Monday. The last one had an unwanted side effect—well, not so much a "side" as a "backside" effect.

I made the connection the second or third week I was back in the field. Every Monday, I got a major case of the runs. Combat is tough enough without self-induced diarrhea and its accompanying cramps.

Just imagine being in the jungle, in the rain, with little or no toilet paper and no underwear, with the galloping cruds, and you'll understand why nobody took their malaria pill on Mondays. A lot of the guys probably didn't take the little white pills the other days either. They wanted malaria. It was a first-class, paid ticket out of combat.

"Here are the malaria pills for your troop for the next month, Smith," said Sgt. T-Rex. "Issue them on Mondays."

"Right, Sarge," I replied, and then thought, 'That's some big bottle. Does it come with a dolly or is it self-propelled?' I knew it would propel something anyway.

I lugged the container of Monday Misery back to my area and deposited it into the nearest available trash can. None of my guys ever got malaria—and on Mondays, none of us left a trail on the trail. Happy Trails!

May 4

    Just got the word this morning: Fred Barkley was shot through the knee while on convoy (armored Jeeps, trucks, etc.) with D Troop. For a while (maybe three days, maybe three months) I'll be assigned to D Troop as their Medic until a replacement arrives.

    Keep writing C Troop Medic on the letters, since I'll be staying in my old tent in the C Troop area and commuting to D Troop. I'm going to try to do as little readjusting as possible!

    The Colonel's chopper was shot at yesterday in the Crescent area. C Troop and I came in on top of a mountain and worked our way down. In the thickets at the base of the hill, a North Vietnamese Army (NVA) soldier with an AK-47 rifle (the type I was wounded with) ran into Rowdy (hospital, Japan) and was killed by the 4th Squad.

    I carried his rifle the rest of the day plus a 30-round banana-type magazine (he didn't have a round in the chamber).

    About it then.

Love, Brad

May 5

    I went out on convoy yesterday with D Troop. I rode on the back of a Jeep carrying a 106mm Recoilless Rifle as part of the escort of four bull-dozers into the An Loa Valley.

    Clearing the road of mines and such, we averaged about 5 mph, but didn't run into anything. I got to load the 106mm when we test fired it.

(l. to r.) Weise, Bratch, and Crew Chief/Door Gunner Betz.

Today, one of the C Troop gunships crashed (shot down by a .51 caliber machine gun), injuring the four crew members (worst was a buddy of mine, Sp/4 Betz, with a compound fracture of the tibia, left leg). Also, a convoy of trucks was headed for LZ English from here at Two Bits, and either our own grenades or VC terrorists killed two GIs and injured several others (one guy, Barnet, from C Troop who rides in my chopper, was very slightly wounded by shrapnel in the side).

Doc Row, who was with C Troop on March 6th when he had seven wounded and Sgt. Kaneshiro was killed, is coming back to 1/9th probably tomorrow. He was shot through the ear. The Flight Surgeon, Capt. Green, says he'll put me back in C Troop (I'm senior to Doc Row and Doc Shore) and put Doc Row in D Troop. I sure hope so!

Later, when Shore is taken out of the field, Row will take his place. Sounds fair enough all the way around.

I carry the rain jacket you sent me in one of my big oversized pants pockets. It folds up to a real convenient size to carry.

It's been a week now since I've had a day off, and I haven't had a shower in ten days or more. I'll be thankful for the rest and the chance to clean up.

Please send the combat photos I took so I can get a look at them. I want some idea of how they came out so I'll know what improvements are needed for future photos.

Those records (especially the Beatles) are great! Sgt. Coung, the interpreter, has me play Frank and Nancy Sinatra on my battery-powered record player every chance I get. He's really sold!

All for now.

Love, Brad

Chapter 33: Top of the World, Ma!

The 1st Cav had a little picnic of pain it called an Artillery Raid.

First, we fired salvos of rounds onto a mountain top as deep into unchallenged enemy territory as our range would allow. Of course, being proponents of "take the high ground," we chose the highest summit for tactical purposes and just because we liked to look down our noses at the neighbors.

After we sufficiently defoliated, de-treed, and leveled the once proud peak, we sent in the picnickers: us, C Troop. We hopped off the helicopters and headed for the "pre-fab" foxholes fashioned by shell craters along the perimeter. Then we waited.

Finally, Chinook helicopters lumbered in carrying the heavyweight stars of the show—105mm howitzers—slung beneath their middle-aged bellies. When a dozen or so were in place, and the ammo stockpiled, coordinates were confirmed and the big guns opened up. All day long they cut loose. And somewhere seven miles east, a Commie command post disappeared or a large troop concentration dissolved into a smaller troop concentrate . . . with pulp. And men who had just finished their lone meager meal of rice and thought they were safe, died in sudden terror and agony.

From our eagle's perch, high explosives rained down on the valley below, unearthed Red Ants and their tunnels with giant spades, and then tossed bodies and dirt to the wind. Nothing was safe within that seven-mile corridor east of our hilltop haven.

Without mercy, we pummeled the valley people: Hobbits and silk-clad Cong, Trolls and terrorists, Gnomes and NVA alike. We buried some alive and blew others apart. Shells fell somewhere every second, as rapid as ten rounds a minute per gun, while we reclined in our holes and relished canned C-rations with a tepid-water chaser. It was indiscriminate death from a distance on a busman's holiday.

I even took the day off. An over-eager new Medic, one who had no formal training but had been pulled from the ranks for on-the-job training, was doing all the work. He asked me to inspect his patients. There were four of them. As the day had progressed, the valley people had lit torches and assembled with pitchforks to storm Frankenstein's Castle. They retraced our cannon's carnage until they knew where we were. As our choppers brought in more ammo and Cs, they also took the occasional stray round. Three guys on board Huey choppers had been hit by the odd fragment. One, however, looked like he'd been shot clean through the cheek. A field dressing covered one entire side of his face. Above the bandages, his eyes betrayed his fear, his apprehension.

"He's the worst one," the novice Medic told me in front of the man and loud enough for everyone to hear.

"And he's not bad off at all," I quickly added, giving the indiscreet baby Doc a silencing look. Then I turned to the seated soldier. "They'll be able to patch you up good as new in Japan," I reassured him. I knelt down to his level. "When they're through, you won't even have a scar."

I didn't know if any of that was true; I only hoped. As I walked away, the new-meat Medic followed. When we were far enough away, I told him, "You did a good job, but . . . you never want to talk about how bad a patient is in front of him. It can destroy his morale and might even throw him into shock."

He nodded and sheepishly said, "OK. Thanks." He was kind of a Baby Huey type, out of shape and fleshy for someone so young. I hoped he would make it. Treating a handful of minor flesh wounds a couple of thousand feet above the enemy was one thing. Running for your collective lives under fire while carrying out a severely wounded man was another. Ninety percent of being a Medic was surviving long enough to do the job.

Life as a Combat Medic boils down to a very black-and-white existence: you either try to save someone or you die trying. There's no middle ground. You don't have time to philosophize about the worth of one individual over the worth of the next. You can't pick and choose your clients. You just get to them anyway you can—mainly by running flat out—and then you . . .

> Check the Airway,
> Stop the Bleeding,
> Protect the Wound,
> Treat for Shock.

That's the life-and-death hand dealt you, and a fifth wild card they don't dwell on much in medical training: Get him out of there! That's the tough one. That's the killer.

At Fort Sam Houston, we trained in teams of five. One of us was on the stretcher and the others carried it. But in combat, there are no stretchers or stretcher bearers. You're it; the whole show. So that fifth wild card often turns into the Joker that separates Medics from the rank-and-file . . . and often separates too many Medics from their lives, their families, and their futures.

On the Vietnam War Memorial, the Black Wall of U.S. KIAs, there are 1,354 names of Medics; 184 of those are from the 1st Cav. For five months in my life, I can honestly say I had the most dangerous job in the world.

With our worn-out welcome and wounded, we packed up our picnic baskets and flew the coop. I have no idea how successful we were or weren't. I only knew none of us died and we had a nice, restful day.

Corporate warfare is a lot like an artillery raid. You storm in with everything you've got, blow the peak off the highest mountain you can find, and set up shop on top. Then you spend your career raining Hell down on those below you—so they can't climb the mountain and take over your position. That's business and that's war—neither lifestyle lasts for long.

Chapter 34: War Zone

"What's a 'War Zone'?" I asked Matt.

"An area we've cleared of all civilians; a Free Fire Zone."

"So, it's Open Season on anybody in there," I said.

"That's right. Anybody crossing a War Zone or found in a War Zone is automatically the enemy."

The first "enemy" they brought me to treat was a seven-year-old boy. He had a gaping hole in the side of his chest, big enough to put my fist through. Time was critical and I knew it. I worked as fast as I could. It took two petroleum gauze dressings to cover it, overlapped, followed by surgical tape to seal it. Finally, I wrapped the whole works with an elastic roller bandage for compression, making sure it wasn't too tight to restrict breathing.

Two of the guys carried him on a chair to the chopper. We turned him over to the door gunner for safe keeping.

"Don't let him lie down!" I shouted over the crescendo of chopper blades. "He has to stay sitting up all the way. Otherwise, he'll drown in his own chest fluids." The crew chief nodded that he understood. Sucking chest wounds were becoming my specialty.

As the gunship-turned-mercy-machine roared off, my spirits soared with it. 'Good work, Brad,' I congratulated myself. 'A good day's work.'

But before I had finished my self-appreciation parade— "Doc's Day"—the Blues brought me another one, a teenage girl, no more than 14. She may have been the boy's big sister for all I knew, and if possible, she was even worse off.

A sizeable hunk of shrapnel had hit her left arm above the elbow. They might just as well have taken a chainsaw to her arm; only a piece of skin the width of my little finger held it on. Whole sections of her arm were spoiled meat or missing entirely.

"Oh, Sweetheart," I said out loud. "Look what they've done to you. I'm so sorry."

She was writhing in pain, but I had to stop the bleeding first. I fished out one of my prized tourniquets from the aid bag, pulled it over her hand and up her arm. I drew it tight enough—remembering the pain I had caused the one VC—and let the metal-spring clasp secure it. That stopped the bleeding, thank God.

Now for the pain. I broke out a morphine syrette and inserted the needle into the deltoid muscle of her good arm.

'Not all of it,' I told myself. 'Just give her two-thirds, three-quarters at the most. She's too small for a full dose.'

I pinned the semi-empty syrette to her blouse, hoping they would see it at the hospital.

Now what? I'd been taught how to wrap the amputated stump of an arm or leg, but how do you treat so much tissue damage with the arm just barely attached? Do I amputate? It would be easy. No! It might throw her into shock.

Instead, I filled the cavity of her upper arm with gauze and then used an elastic bandage for compression. Good, but something was missing: a sling!

I pulled out a cravat triangular bandage—prized for its versatility—placed half of it between her body and arm, and folded the other half over her arm. Then I knotted it behind her neck. Now, she would at least *think* she would keep her arm.

By now the morphine had kicked in and she was quiet.

The tall Lieutenant stood over us. Without looking up at him, I said, "That's it. All we can do for her now is to get her out of here."

I must have hit a nerve or something. With all the venom of one of those village pit vipers, he roared,

"I know you're the great humanitarian, Doc, but we can't stop the war for one little girl!"

I was shocked. I wanted to ask, 'Why not? It seems like the perfect excuse to stop this stupid war to me!'

Instead, I said, "I'm sorry, Sir. I wasn't saying we had to fly her out, I was just saying that's all I can do for her."

"Oh," he said. Then he radioed upstairs to evac her out. He really wasn't such a bad guy, for an Officer.

When I finished, Sgt. Henley told me, "Doc, I wouldn't trade jobs with you for all the money in the world!"

Seeing kids all chewed up like that had really drained me and I was spent. Of course, the war wasn't. It went on—even if I felt I'd already earned my combat pay for the whole month in one morning. I soon discovered this was only the Children's Hour: AM Pediatrics. Adult Sick Call waited in the wings.

Some hours later, the War Zone actually coughed up a real enemy soldier who met the age requirement and everything. He was big for a Vietnamese, close to my height of 6' and my size. Again, shrapnel had done its gruesome job—mangling the calf of his left leg and right foot. I wrapped him up—no tourniquet this time—and administered morphine. Then things got interesting.

"I'll take him to the chopper for you, Doc," said Clay. Now Corporal Clay was about 6' 3", 210 pounds, with a Fu Manchu mustache. Even in his neighborhood back home he carried a .32 revolver. He scared me and I knew him!

With one swoop, he picked the NVA up in his arms. Of course, the wounded man had never seen anybody or anything as big and scary as Clay in his whole life. He grabbed me around the neck in a death grip. Clay pried his fingers loose and carried him to the waiting chopper like a baby. I still remember the NVA's eyes pleading with me as the two of them left.

Later, I found out that the wounded man had been a 20-year NVA veteran squad leader. He was grateful because we didn't kill him—maybe he thought Clay would eat him—and for the treatment I gave him and the Army hospital follow up. He was so grateful, in fact, that he "spilled his guts" about NVA movements, troop concentrations, and strategic plans.

How many American lives were saved by that one act of compassion?

That night, Matt came into my tent. "I just got back from 67th Evac, and I thought you'd like to know that both of those kids you treated today are going to make it."

"Great!" I said, smiling. "Thanks for telling me. I really appreciate it."

"You know, Doc," Matt continued, "in my eyes, you'll always wear a little halo for what you did today."

Lesson #11: War is what you make of it. It doesn't have to be a private Hell.

141

Chapter 35: Souvenirs

When I was a second grader, a little girl brought in something special for "Show and Tell." Her dad had been a paratrooper with the 101st Airborne. They were the first unit to enter Hitler's lair at Burchess Garden on top of a peak of the Bavarian Alps.

For a souvenir, each member of his squad took a key they found hanging on pegs on the wall. Her dad got the key to Hitler's restroom.

The teacher passed it down the rows in class so we could all handle it. The key was large, ornate, heavy, and filled my small grade-school hand. I touched it and turned it over. 'Every time Hitler took a dump,' I thought, 'he used this key.' Later, I learned that he dumped excessively and often on humanity without it.

Ho Chi Minh probably didn't even use a toilet, let alone have a key to one. One time in Qui Nhon, I saw an old man squat right on the beach and unload. Could have been Ho on R&R . . . no, really.

My cousin was a "Sergeant of the Gun" with a 175mm mobile artillery unit in Nam after I left country. At nights, he pulled patrols outside the parameter. As he was packing up to come home, he grabbed two live hand grenades for souvenirs and stuffed them into the depths of his duffel.

Years later, when his two sons got to the curtain-climber and yard-ape stage, he started to think about the prospect of his prying brood blowing up half his house and all his family. So one hot, summer night, he took his souvenirs to a field outside his hometown, pulled the pins, and let them fly. It was the Fourth of July. Happy Birthday, America.

When the 1st Cav originally began operations in 1965, Troopers could keep automatic weapons they captured. This was soon downgraded to semi-automatic rifles. By the time I arrived, we could only send bolt-action rifles home. One of our number captured an AK that he neglected to turn in. Back in his tent, he stripped the weapon down to its key components and shipped them home—one piece at a time—over several months. I've heard of guys in the Motor Pool doing the same thing with Jeeps.

My souvenir collection was less dramatic. When C Troop captured weapons, they would often give them to me to carry. I always pulled the magazines and emptied the chambers—then slipped one round into my pocket from each type of weapon. I ended up with shells from an AK-47, M-1 Carbine, M-1 Garand, an armor-piercing shell from a German Mauser, a small shell from the drum magazine of a World War II Russian burp gun, and even a round from a MAT-49 sub-machine gun captured from the French. I also managed to fit one of my aid bags—minus the morphine—into my duffel bag, along with a couple of fatigue shirts. I wish I'd kept my helmet, too.

Chapter 36: The House

From a distance, shrouded in the early morning haze rising from the valley, it looked like home. Tile roof. Stucco walls. Ranch-style architecture. A little piece of Southern California dropped into the arm pit of Southern Vietnam.

"Matt," I said, "is that really a house over there? No thatched roof. No bamboo frame. No palm branch walls. I mean a real, live stateside house?"

"Looks like it, Doc."

"Weird, isn't it? I mean 'Twilight Zone' weird. What's it doing in the middle of a War Zone?"

"Might be left over from the French," Matt said, "when they occupied Vietnam . . . before the Japanese came and left . . . and the French came back after World War II . . .then left for good after Dien Bien Phu."

"Sounds like a lot of traffic through these parts, Matt."

We left the mystery house behind as we began to climb a neighboring hill, our mission for the day. A nosey chopper crew had spotted suspicious signs of activity near its peak.

Halfway up, even hotter and sweatier than usual because of the climb, the current resident caught us trespassing. He unleashed the dogs of war on us, those that barked death:

"Crack! Crack! Crack!"

We came back down the hill. There was no impassioned order to "Fix bayonets! Charge!" Most of us didn't even carry a bayonet. Unlike the Marines or Teddy Roosevelt, we never took hills, at least not from the bottom up. We were exclusively high-ground Troopers and, being the 1st Air Cav, we always held the highest ground.

Time to call in the United States Air Force! "Off we go into the wild blue yonder."

The house wasn't an illusion after all. While we waited for the F-105s to arrive, we took up temporary residence there. Once inside, envy entered the equation, voiced by a C Troop chorus:

"Cement floors! It's even got cement floors!"

"They're living better than we are."

"Why they're living better than my folks—this tile roof is nicer than ours back home."

144

"This just ain't right."

And it wasn't. In retrospect, I think the house represented the disparity of our times. Stateside, Fat Cats were living high, dry, and safe; while in Nam, Cat Troop slept in leaky tents, ate out of OD cans, and played Russian roulette with our lives. So maybe in some futile gesture of defiance, Matt and I looked at each other and, in unison, said, "Let's burn it down!"

We gathered brush and branches, broken chairs, and anything else that would burn. We stacked them throughout the house, in each of the six rooms, and then saturated the heaps of debris with insect repellent.

"OK, let's move out," came the Lieutenant's order. "We'll cross the 300 yards to that ravine over there and take cover."

As C Troop vacated the premises, Matt touched off the bonfires with his trusty Zippo lighter. We were the last to leave.

Just as the house mimicked California, so did the ravine and its stream. They reminded me of the Creek back home. 'Here I am,' I reflected, '20 years old and still playing at war.'

If I was still playing at war, the Air Force wasn't. Big flying gas tank F-105 fighter-bombers—"Thunder Chiefs"—rumbled into action. They were so ugly that they were beautiful, especially to an infantryman.

Fifteen minutes later, from the safety of the ravine, we had two shows to watch: the burning house and the erupting mountain.

145

You had to admire that lone VC though. As the F-105s made their run, you could hear his AK snap at them. Then they'd drop a 750-pound iron bomb and the world exploded. Still, as soon as the plane pulled up—"Crack! Crack! Crack!"—he'd be right back in their face. Cock-eyed Commie Optimist.

I could almost picture him sitting on top of his log and earth bunker, elbows propped on his knees, shoulder to his weapon, peppering away—with no chance of ever downing a jet. He was either brave beyond reason, stoned out of his mind, or both. We were almost rooting for him. When his AK finally did fall silent, so did we.

Still, the big planes pounded the simple mountain lair, seeing how high they could bounce the rubble—and his remains—with Mom and Dad's tax dollars.

Even at 300 yards away, shrapnel splashed 30 feet below us in the ravine's stream—big, honkin' pieces of shrapnel. The whole Troop sat at the top of the ridge like kids in the cheap seats at a Dodger game in Chavez Ravine.

I watched for a while from those same seats, long enough to see the roof cave in on our house. It was awesome, an arsonist's dream, but not worth dying for.

"Hey," I said. "There's shrapnel flying right past us and hitting the river. This isn't a safe place to be."

All I heard in return was, "Yeah, Doc" and "Sure, Doc." No one budged. Maybe they'd forgotten what shrapnel did to those two kids the week before, the last time we crossed into a War Zone. I hadn't forgotten; I never would.

Finally, only Marty, Tong, and I went down the slope to the river.

"Did you see that?!" someone shouted above us. "It uprooted that whole tree and blew it 200 feet straight up!"

'Sorry I missed that one, but if I get hit again, who's going to patch up you sports fans? Besides, I'm kind of attached to my face and I'd like to keep it that way—attached.'

The F-105s wagged their wings and double-clutched their engines to say goodbye, our signal to leave our box seats, cross the dry field, and climb the still smoldering hill.

At the Mount St. Helens summit, or what was left of it, the landscape resembled the crater of a volcano. No body. No bunker. Nothing was left.

It reminded me of my first Arc Light mission, eight months before. We climbed another hill, covered with thick jungle. Suddenly, the green trees turned gray-brown, stripped of their limbs and leaves. Another few yards, and we were in a clearing.

"Look at this," I said to one of the many Blues I didn't know at the time. "How do you think this clearing got out here in the middle of the jungle?"

The other soldier looked at me like I was yesterday's C-rations. He said, "It's a crater from a 1,000-pound bomb, Doc, dropped from a B-52. That's what an Arc Light mission is: we check them out for casualties and report back."

"Oh," I said, and then felt like adding, 'Got any booby traps I can swing from?'

May 14—While returning to Base Camp after a day of patrolling, we were diverted to an area where our gunships had just fired on three personnel running in a field. We arrived, "hot" LZ and all. One NVA was dead, shot through the head—the other was either dead or dying, having muscle spasms. He had been hit in the abdomen exposing his entrails. I tried to save him, but he had already gone into shock.

A young Viet Cong boy with them was unhurt and we took him alive.

The last two days I've had gastroenteritis from handling the NVA's intestines. I guess I didn't wash my hands well enough before I ate that night. I'm fine now, though, so don't worry.

As an instrument of God's will and tender mercy, I've been able to save three lives since I came here seven months ago. I have no fear of the future as my trust is in the Almighty.

All for now.

Love, Brad

May 17

Sorry I haven't written in a while, but maybe you'll understand why after I tell you what's been happening.

The day Fred Barkley was wounded by a sniper with an AK-47 Assault Rifle, C Troop killed the very same sniper (about 2 hours later). I was along that day, and went to D Troop the very next.

I was with D Troop on convoy missions for a week. The last day a woman flagged us down. Her little boy had been playing and tripped a VC Booby-Trapped Grenade. His groin had been peppered with shrapnel, but I don't believe he was that seriously injured. The woman had panicked and without regard for her son's still bleeding wounds, she had carried him the mile to the road. Needless to say, he had bled to death by the time I got to him.

The next day, I was back with C Troop and going out every day. We were flying toward our mission areas, when we sighted a crippled chopper in trouble. It was a 5/7th Cav gunship spinning, diving straight down sometimes, and finally crashing. We came in fast and I got to the wounded. Through God's mercy, only one man suffered a possible broken back and bloody nose. I wrapped up his chest to give him as much support (spine and ribs) as possible and evacuated him out.

That afternoon while on Recon of the Southern An Loa (cave and rock region), we found an NVA with head, face, and hip wounds from artillery rounds. We carried him out of the cave into an open rice paddy.

I had just finished dressing his wounds when one or more snipers opened up on us. We took cover and returned fired. We succeeded in withdrawing from hedgerow to hedgerow until we were safely out of range (Artillery and Gunships blasted the area all night long).

In the following few days, we made continual contacts, killing at least one VC or NVA per day and capturing several more.

May 21

Just put in for R&R. For first choice, I asked for Australia; second choice, Hawaii. Since I have seven months in country, it should come through in a month or two. I'll write you in a while to send a money order for $300. That should be more than enough to cover expenses.

I'll tell Emily to drop by for the pictures and just to talk.

About it for now.

Love, Brad

May 30 & 31

We sacked up a VC yesterday in a cave and found another dead.

In 45-60 days, I should be out of combat and in An Khe (rear area). This is about a month to 1½ months earlier than I expected. Right now, I'm the longest lived (combat time) Medic in 1/9th Cav.

No pipe yet, or film, but should get them soon.

Hard to write going out every day like this. Should have an alternate Medic again before long.

That's it then.

Love to All, Brad

Chapter 37: Milk Run

"We're flying out to set up a perimeter around a downed chopper," I told the two guys new to the Troop. They looked unduly concerned, like it might prove fatal or something for them. "It's no big deal," I tried to reassure them. "It's a milk run."

We laid behind the dry paddy dike waiting for the flying tow truck, the two-propped Chinook helicopter, to join us overhead. That's when the first shot hit Rick in the side of the chest.

"Medic!"

I scurried across the cracked earth on all fours, keeping as low as I could, using muscles in strange new ways that would hurt for the next week.

Rick was a draftee. He didn't want to be in Nam, and if you talked with him at any length, he'd tell you that he wasn't going to make it home.

By the time I finished my crab crawl, those closest to Rick had him on his back with his chest exposed. The entry wound didn't look that serious; but there was no exit wound and Rick was incoherent.

I dressed the wound—petroleum gauze and surgical tape—while he mumbled. Then he stopped breathing. I gave him chest compressions and mouth-to-mouth, gagging as I finished. Nothing. The bullet had found his heart.

Rick was big, so four of us carried him to the chopper. "He's dead," I told the Crew Chief. I still had the taste of his last breath in my mouth.

We laid low behind the dikes as our choppers chewed up the countryside. Things must have gotten confused for the late arrivals in the holding pattern above:

"Guess what?" one Radioman said. "They think we're an artillery unit down here."

"And I'm a 105mm Howitzer," I replied, beginning to lose it. "Kaboom! Kaboom!" I said. Two of the guys nearby looked a little uneasily at me. I shut up.

Word was we were going to sweep the village where the shots came from that killed Rick. This was not going to be pretty.

One VC tried to hide in a water wheel along the river. When we spotted him and opened fire, he dove in and held his breath.

Nam's man hunters waited patiently for him to resurface. When he did, gasping for air, they stitched him up the front with their M-16s. There would be no prisoners this day.

While all this was happening, I was up to my armpits in trouble, literally. I stepped onto a dike or ridge of some kind, only to have it cave in underneath me. I fell through with only my arms stopping me.

"Marty!" I called in a hushed voice. "Marty!"

He turned, saw just my head and arms, and dropped his jaw. He rushed over to help.

I felt strangely suspended somehow between Heaven and Hell. I wasn't wet, so it couldn't be a sewer, yet it was deep enough so that I couldn't touch bottom. Where was I?

Then it dawned on me: I was hanging like some sorry-looking chandelier inside a Viet Cong tunnel! And they could do anything they liked to me; anything and nothing I wanted to think about at the moment. 'Ho, look what just dropped in: half a Medic. Care to split the bounty with me?'

When Marty pulled my sad sack out of there, I could have hugged him.

C Troop killed ten VC that day and five more over the next two days. Other Cav units netted another 84 KIAs. Still, none of that brought back Rick.

Lesson #12: In war, there is no good way to die.

Chapter 38: Down Days

Down Days were the best days. I remember one in particular. . . .

It was hot, above 100 degrees, with humidity close behind. There were a lot of days like that in the Nam. When it was that hot, no one felt much like eating, so we headed for the artillery area of the base. There they had Cokes in real ice for a dime apiece.

(l. tor r.): Bratch, Marty, Charles, and Me at Graveyard LZ Two Bits.

Marty, Bratch, Weise, and I all bought a Coke with our Monopoly military scrip and pulled up four available lawn chairs they had under a tent awning. We were in heaven. The Cokes were so cold and good that we returned nine more times that day, each time drinking another ice-cold Coca Cola. We didn't even eat that day, we just drank Cokes.

Maybe it was the caffeine, but in between one of our Coke runs someone started a rock fight. As if we didn't see enough combat, on our day off we ended up throwing rocks at each other. About a dozen of us ran between the tents and ducked behind trees with all the expertise and agility of hardened veterans.

I hit the Forward Observer, Matt, in the chest with a well-placed shot. He looked shocked, his expression saying, 'But you're a Medic.'

I threw another, regular-sized rock at Bratch. He retaliated by picking up a big one and heaving it at me. I only just managed to step out of its way. Now I was the one with the surprised look.

"That's how it's done, Doc," said Bratch, a kind of Jimmy Stewart type. "Someone throws a rock at you; you find the biggest one you can and throw it back."

Yeah, that's how it's done.

June 14

Hard to write—nothing worth repeating—the days' events get uglier and uglier.

The only consolation is I have a very good chance of being permanently taken out of the field and combat in about 30 days! My tour of combat would be through and I have a better than even chance of being sent back to the hospital in Japan for continued therapy on my arm for the last three months of my tour.

Looks like I'll be out of C Troop and the country when we move to a different area of operations.

The summer monsoons are upon us and the Cav is as wet as wet can be.

Got my pipe the other day—that pre-smoked idea is pretty good. Thanks.

Another thing—if I get to go to Japan, I can workout, eat properly, and gain all my weight back.

Quiet now, waiting to saddle-up.

I'll write again soon.

Love, Brad

June 17

Made an LZ across the river from Two Bits and picked up two 9mm French MAT-49 submachine guns Charlie had taken from the French after 1949.

Remember Rowdy from Fort Wayne, Indiana? He's up for sergeant and 4th squad leader. Good chance of getting it, too.

Sgt. Matt (photos) left for home today—glad he made it, but hated to see him go.

Just got word I have an insured package in An Khe. I've just mailed the permit slip authorizing the mail clerk to send it out. Might be my film for the camera.

We're working an isolated section of the An Loa—Montagnard country. You could almost live there. I'll get some good shots of it.

Big ARVN operation in the Crows Foot today. We probably won't be needed.

About it then.

Love, Brad

Chapter 39: Life at the Wire

Mama san

There existed a world within the war, one inhabited by the munchkin people of South Vietnam, supposedly the reason behind "Why We Fight." For a lot of bored young men like me, this world away waited on the other side of the perimeter wire.

No gate separated our two worlds, theirs and ours, only a zigzag snake of 15-foot high Constantino wire. The roll upon roll of thorns without the roses was like something out of Alice's croquet match. A bunker and M-60 overlooked the maze, its finger-fed burst barring the way to the uninvited by promising to open another gate to the Hereafter.

Helmetless and with our M-16s nonchalantly slung over our shoulders, we walked the gauntlet back and forth whenever we could.

"Hi, Doc!" one kid greeted me, and then politely asked, "You bring candy?" Aw, yes, candy . . . the same in any language, any culture . . . just like children.

"Sorry," I said. "Fresh out. I bring next time."

"Tomorrow?" he asked.

"No tomorrow. Next time I come. Tomorrow I hunt your Uncle Charlie." The Trooper next to me laughed.

The boy smiled and said, "OK, Doc, next time."

The kids at the wire were pretty decent, for Vietnamese kids. They weren't like the boys and girls in town who tried to steal the ammo magazines out of your rifle as they crowded around you, or anything else they could get their grubby little hands on. The kids at the wire were our kids, they deserved candy. I made a mental note to fill my fatigue pant pockets full "next time."

Apart from the children's hour at the wire, a soap opera of sorts played out for adult audiences. One G.I. sat with a teenage girl, their eyes and body language, punctuated by butchered English and battered Vietnamese words, conjured up memories of high school romances. She was in love; he was in heat, as SSgt. Fester so poetically phrased it.

"Where Johnson?" another young woman asked about her boyfriend.

"Gone home," a Trooper told her. He seemed to take pleasure in her pained expression. "No come back."

The arms of friends enveloped her as the light left once bright eyes. Her Johnson hadn't even said good bye. So much for love in the afternoon—outside a graveyard—not worth Two Bits.

Charlie eluded us again, and it was my promised candy-delivery day down at the wire. I dutifully lined my pockets with hard treats and braved the prickly path to kids' land.

The minute I stepped into the open, half a dozen hooch Hobbits tackled me. I passed out candy until my olive-drab cupboards were bare. As they scurried off with their prizes, I smiled. I'd done a good thing. That's when Charlie's Nephew showed up . . . late. With both his hands out, he looked at me with all the anticipation of any child in any country.

"You were late," I said. "I brought candy, but it all gone." His face fell. "I'm sorry, but the other kids got to it first." Then he started trying to go through my pockets.

"Hey, knock it off! I told you, it's all gone. Stop it! I don't have any more." I shoved him. His eyes were as empty as his hands as he walked away.

Ten minutes later, I had put the incident out of my mind when something hard hit me in the small of the back: a rock! I turned to see Charlie's Nephew throw another one at me from 20 feet away. This time I managed to dodge the malevolent missile.

"You number ten, Doc! You no bring candy you promise!" My pint-sized assassin reached for another rock, but I half hurled one at him first, thumping him in the chest. Bratch had schooled me well. I controlled the force of my throw, but not that of my words,

"You don't throw rocks at me! Who do you think you are? I came here to save your lousy country!"

The sugar-free Nephew withdrew unharmed. I was afraid I'd lost a friend—even if he was a hard-candy-bribed one.

Hero worship in a war can be hazardous to your health, even more so than too much sugar, especially if you're a kid. On yet another trip to the world outside the wire, two boys came up to us sporting a couple of hand-made toys. They were roughly hewn from local wood and painted black.

One kid held his prize next to my rifle to see if they'd gotten the dimensions right. Then he smiled and said something unintelligible to his friend who smiled back. They were obviously pleased with their work.

As they left, I said to a Trooper next to me, "I sure hope they don't cross any rice paddies with those things. From a distance, they look just like M-16s."

The Trooper nodded his head and replied, "Yeah, I know. Our choppers would nail them for sure."

I wished I could have warned them, but language was always a barrier anywhere in Nam.

At least the war games I played at their age weren't potentially as lethal. Of course, I did just miss hitting my sister Jody with an arrow one day; but what's a sister for?

One of our choppers did accidentally shoot a farmer's son while we were on patrol. The pilot landed and offered the grieving father $20. The man's whole countenance changed. He smiled through his tears, took the bills, and bowed several times. He had other children, but little money. Life is cheap in a war—and negotiable.

Pot was even cheaper. The locals handed out free cigarettes at the wire. I smoked them a few times, but evidently didn't have the necessary genes in my biological makeup to enjoy the experience. Instead of euphoria, marijuana just made me angry. Alcohol made me sick. Even the drugs the doctors administered prior to my several surgeries made me puke.

I guess I don't have the stomach for such things. Strange, isn't it, how you can have the stomach for handling exposed entrails, severed limbs, sucking chest wounds, and otherwise mangled bodies, and yet not be able to hold your liquor? It's like we're given the things we need and not those we don't need. It's just a matter of figuring out where those gifts fit into the Big HD Flat Screen of Life.

I never knew if the free pot was a public relations ploy to encourage us to buy more or a Commie means to take the edge off our fighting ability. I heard of guys who smoked a joint in the helicopters on the way to a mission. I napped.

In retrospect, our friends at the wire may not have been all that friendly. We found out later that our barber, who often followed us onto the base for haircuts, was in truth a VC. He seemed like a nice enough guy, though when I asked for a haircut one day like Bratch's, he gave me a butch instead. At least it was cooler under my helmet.

I even got a shave once—with a straight razor, no less— when there was an explosion nearby. The sudden loud noise might have made the barber shave me closer than he—or I—liked! Young and dumb.

Another time, a young girl's questions about one of our guys who had just died seemed odd. Was she genuinely interested or was she just gathering intelligence for her VC boyfriend?

Then there was "Two-Wheeled Charlie" who we spotted in broad daylight walking his bike around the outside of the perimeter. It was obvious that he was pacing off the distance between our bunkers pending an attack. For whatever reasons at the time, we let him.

My last trip down to the wire, when I knew I'd be leaving Nam any day now, seemed like it was right out of a Norman Rockwell painting.

"Doc, you go back America?" It was Charlie's Nephew, the one who traded hard rocks, and harder words, for hard candy with me.

"Yeah," I replied. "Soon."

As I started to walk back to the entrance to the base, the boy took my hand and walked me to the wire. Then he said, "Thank you come to Vietnam. My father thank you. My mother thank you. My sister thank you. I thank you."

It may have smacked of George M. Cohan and "Yankee Doodle Dandy," but his words touched me. Little did I know that it would be the only thanks I'd hear for more than 20 years!

After all those years, the next time someone thanked me for going to war, they were *again* Vietnamese—this time a couple standing in a buffet line behind me. Of course, now they were Americans, too. I recognized their distinctive speech patterns. Hearing a local speak Vietnamese still sends the hairs bristling on the back of my neck. I turned and spoke to them. When I mentioned I'd been in Vietnam during the war, they smiled, nodded, and thanked me. All I could find to say to them in reply was, "I'm sorry we lost your country."

"I'm sorry we lost your country"—have you ever heard anything more pathetic? 'Sorry you don't have a home anymore. Sorry you'll never see the rest of your family again. Sorry we let thugs kill your aunt, uncle, brother, sister, mom, or dad. Sorry we failed you . . . and ourselves. Sorry for the friends we lost over there.' Pathetic!

The first time I heard Americans publicly show gratitude for our sacrifice was at a Billy Graham Crusade in Anaheim, California, in the 1980s. The guest speaker who warmed up the audience before Dr. Graham spoke was a Vietnam Vet himself, his face horribly disfigured from burns, but his spirit glowing through the scar tissue. After he related his own story about the war, he stopped and said, "It's long past time to thank our Vietnam veterans for what they did over there for us. If you're a veteran of that war, would you please stand."

Accustomed to looks of disdain and comments like "baby killer" and "you got what you deserved," the several score of us there reluctantly rose to our feet. Angel Stadium erupted in salvos of applause—long and sustained. I felt like I'd finally come home.

Chapter 40: Quick Reaction

C Troop was a Quick Reaction Force. That meant we had to be ready to saddle up at any time, night or day, with only five minutes' notice. One day, I wasn't ready.

On my way back from the Med Supply Tent, I saw "slicks" emblazoned with yellow circles flying low overhead. C Troop! They were leaving for a mission—and possibly combat—without a Medic: Me!

I ran to the Flight Ops tent, "I'm Doc Smith. C Troop just took off without me. Can you get me on a chopper?"

I knew if the Blues hit anything serious, there would be no one there to treat the wounded. Men might die and, to make matters worse, I could be facing a General Court Marshal, maybe even hard time at Leavenworth.

"It's OK, Doc," said a staff sergeant. "It was a downed chopper, but another unit in the area said they'd take care of it. C Troop is on its way back in."

C Troop never, I mean never, turned back for any reason, period. That day, the unit pinch-hitting for us ran into the same superior NVA force that had shot down our helicopter. They suffered 5 KIA and 15 WIA. That unit could have been C Troop—without me!

Much later, I found out that their Medic—Edgar McWethy—received the Medal of Honor for his efforts that day. It was awarded posthumously!

Once again, I felt as if Someone—with a whole lot of clout—was watching my back.

The 1/9th gunship took a bellyful of 12.7mm AA machine gun fire as it flew low to check out suspicious activity. Before it crashed into the hard soil, it flipped over. All four crewmen were killed. I knew one of them, Sgt. Walker.

Walker looked the part; he looked like you'd think a soldier ought to look. He was built like a middleweight boxer, but with rugged good looks, not ravaged. When the Cav first arrived in Nam—when things were really hairy—he had been a Squad Leader. He was about ten times tougher than I was or ever would be.

Now he was a smoldering corpse.

"Doc, when we go back out to secure the chopper, you'll be giving Graves Registration a hand," said the Lieutenant.

"Yes, Sir," I said . . . 'love to, looking forward to it.'

When we landed and approached the burned-out hulk, my temporary assignment changed.

"Graves Registration is a no show. You're it, Doc."

Along with several others who had been "volunteered" to help, I put on heavy work gloves. Then we all stood just looking at the wreck, without moving. It was only barely recognizable as a helicopter. The bodies that protruded from underneath the charred remains were unrecognizable, period. But they were our friends.

We stood there awhile longer, until I realized everyone else was waiting for me to make the first move. I walked over, leaned down, and grabbed a charcoal-black body under the armpits. When I pulled, his body came out, but his legs stayed under the debris. Grizzly.

By the position of their arms and torsos, I took them to be the pilot and copilot. They had been trying to crawl out from the wreckage when they were burned to death.

We found dog tags on one and a wallet on the other for positive I.D. We gently placed the bodies onto a poncho. The cooked blood that pooled on the green plastic looked like the drippings from a rare steak. For years thereafter, I only ate my meat well done.

We pulled out another body with tags. That left only Sgt. Walker.

Me (l.) with the remains of Sgt. Walker. Two other working troopers unidentified.
Photo courtesy of Matthew Brennan, author of *FLASHING SABER*.

I found him near remains of the machine gun. The heat of the turbine engine and its JP-4 fuel must have reached its hottest temperatures where he died. I only managed to retrieve his head attached to part of his chest. The rest of his boxer's body was fused with the aluminum airframe. I carried out the once muscular, rugged sergeant in a poncho with one hand. He was still more of a man than I was.

We loaded the remains of our friends and fellow troopers onto a chopper, climbed aboard, and took off. The downed chopper looked like a fly speck on the windshield of the countryside below.

In 15 minutes, we landed at the Graves Registration LZ to drop off the bodies. One of the Graves guys who took the ponchos from us looked distressed, like he might upchuck or cry or something. Those of us on the chopper just stared. We said nothing to him or to one another. We didn't speak the rest of the way back to Two Bits—and we never talked about the crash or Sgt. Walker again.

We killed more than 80 enemy in the action that followed. It didn't make up for Rick and it wasn't enough for Walker, either. It never is.

163

June 23

Today we were working the area around LZ Hammond (my home before December 1st), when a chopper was downed. Air strikes by our jets really brought some hurt on "Charlie." Out with a four-man Combat Tracker Team—all Airborne Rangers working with dogs. Very grungy and tough—make us look like amateurs, but not much.

June 24 & 25

Stand-down two days this week—days off for all concerned. We were watching a movie last night—Cavalry vs. the Indians— when a sniper opened up with an AK-47. We all hit the dirt or scattered. Those realistic war movies just aren't my cup of tea!

Capt. Green, our Flight Surgeon (MD), examined my hand and told me he was sending me to the hospital in Qui Nhon to see a Nerve Specialist. From there it will probably be Japan for the remainder of my tour. Only 3-4 more days and I'll be out of the field for good and all.

That's it then.

Love, Brad

Post Script

We were lying on the airstrip watching the movie on an improvised sheet screen when the sniper opened up. We took off so fast we ran over the film projector and broke it. By the time we stopped running, we were all out of breath. All that walking and hiking and I'm still out of shape? I looked at Bratch who was puffing away, too.

"Humpin' the boonies only gets you into condition for humpin' the boonies," he said. "That's all it's good for."

June 27

A photographer and Army war correspondent are doing a story on me—"Man Without a Weapon"—or something like that for the Army newspaper. He has one photo of the 1st Cav Division Commander standing over me while I patched up that NVA soldier.

Today, we awoke at 3:30 am and took off at 4:15 am to surround a village while the National Police (Vietnamese) swept it for Cong. Nothing came of it.

Capt. Green is making an appointment for me in Qui Nhon (hospital). Shouldn't be long before I leave. All packed now and ready to move. No Australian R&R, but I'll make up for it in Japan. Good to be alive—93 degrees and breezy.

Love, Brad

Chapter 41: Fourth of July

In 1967, the Fourth of July came early for C Troop—a week early, on June 28. The village of An Quang in the Crescent along the South China Sea threw us their version of an Independence Day celebration. They put up a sign that read, "This Village Welcomes the Viet Cong." We took it as an open invitation to bring the fireworks.

Party goers that we were, we landed on a sandy isthmus jutting out into an inland lake known as Dam Tra-O, along the coast of the South China Sea. It was a finger of land—no doubt the middle finger—just wide enough for our choppers to drop off the Blues' four squads.

We passed by the "Welcome" sign, a real work of art of bricks plastered over in white with colored Vietnamese words. Nice job. Guess they meant it.

Old movies used to have a line: "It was quiet . . . too quiet." For a Recon troop that depends on a high degree of stealth pursuing guerrillas who live or die by their stealthiness, it's always too quiet.

The only hint of anything to come was one man with his whole family and their possessions in the middle of the lake. He was paddling away from us and the village as if their lives depended on it. They did.

"Look at that guy," I said to no one in particular. "Where does he think he's going?"

We edged our way up the sandy digit toward the village. The rows of Prickly Pear cactus reminded me of California and home. I was getting "short" and everything reminded me of home now.

Then the war reminded me I wasn't home quite yet.

"Crack! Crack! Crack! Crack!"

As one, the two dozen of us dropped down like marionettes whose strings had been sliced clean with one stroke of a razor. In the sand, I concentrated on getting as low as I could, like a pregnant sea turtle scooping out a hole with its flippers to lay its eggs. My goal was to crawl up inside my helmet until only my jungle boots stuck out. 'Become one with the helmet; one with the sand.' That's when I realized I was alone!

"Hey, Doc," I heard Sgt. Haskett call from the other side of

166

the cactus row. "Are you all right?"

"Yeah, Sarge."

"Then how would you like to join the rest of us?" I heard a couple of the others laugh.

"Yeah, I would."

"OK, then come on over."

"OK," I said. "Here I come. I'm coming over now. Don't shoot me!"

I dove over the row of Prickly Pear and landed with a thud. Everything made it over except my pride.

"Glad you could join us, Doc," said Haskett wryly.

Now C Troop switched occupations as the rest of the Cav was called in. We would take on the role of a blocking force in case the enemy tried to escape down the finger.

Over the next hour, the ground troops of the 1st Air Cav surrounded the village. Over the next 36 hours, 32 air strikes and some 3,000 artillery shells rained down on VC and villager alike—courtesy of the combined forces of the United States Navy, Air Force, and Army. The placid hamlet would pay a horrible price for its insolence, and I would be there to pick up the change. Happy 4th.

Those air strikes and artillery rounds took time to deliver results, to drive out the VC and create a new crop of civilian wounded, so we just lay in the sand and baked.

The new FO, who had replaced Matt, did a better job of baking than most. His age, in his 30s; and his weight, in the 200s; led to heat prostration. Marty, his radio operator, was with him. Marty looked at me. We both looked at the FO. He was too old and fat to be in combat. I knew what Marty was thinking; we were both thinking it, 'He's no Matt.'

I made sure he got enough water and a wet bandanna to cool his head. He recovered without needing to evac him out. My next patient was another matter. We called him "Squirrel."

"Doc, would you look at this?" he asked. "I got something in my finger."

My diagnosis took two seconds, "You've been hit by shrapnel." It was under the skin, but no bleeding. "Go get on a chopper and have them take you to the Evac Hospital."

Two hours later, I saw Squirrel walking around.

167

"Are you back already?" I asked.

"No, Doc," he said, "I never went. It was just a scratch."

Now, as usual, I'll edit my response for the sake of brevity and for the sensitive ears of anyone under the age of 117. "Are *you* the Medic?" I yelled. "Do I look like I'm out here for my health? I outrank you, too. Shrapnel is made of lead. If you don't get it out of your finger it will enter your blood stream. It will poison you. Now go get your fat can on that chopper!"

With the encouragement of one of the sergeants, Squirrel left.

The shadows were lengthening. I decided that the VC welcome sign was too substantial to go to waste, so I staked out the spot behind the sign for the night. With my aid bags as pillows, I curled up into a prenatal ball behind it. Soon, it was dusk.

Then I heard an unfamiliar sound for Vietnam: the welcome rumbling of armor! It was an M-48 Patton tank with a 90mm gun; a throwback to World War II and Korea. Later I found out it belonged to the 1/69th Armored Regiment, the Black Panthers. It came over a large sand dune about 300 yards in the distance.

'Tanks!' I thought. 'Now we're cookin'; we've got armored support—just like World War II.'

Just then, my armored guardian angel stopped dead, and a flame shot up from the top of the turret, like the flick of a *BIC* lighter. The VC had knocked out our tank with an RPG-7—a Russian Rocket-Propelled Grenade!

Two or three minutes later, another M-48 followed in its tracks. Another flame erupted from its top. Another crew of four men died a horrible, blazing death, cooked alive by a white-hot blast of molten metal. No sound. No explosion. No screams. Just eight dead Americans.

A close friend and restaurant co-worker of my dad's had a son in armor somewhere in Nam. He was a captain and talk was that I might meet up with him one day. Maybe I did, and didn't know it. I heard much later that he had been killed in much the same way.

I curled up into an even tighter ball behind my brick-and-plaster billboard and tried to go to sleep. Soon I was no longer in Vietnam; no longer in a war.

Lesson #13: There are no safe havens in war—up in the sky; under the waves; behind steal, concrete, or rocks.

That night, a dozen VC tried to make a break for it. They chose to come down the finger and through C Troop. They chose wrong.

The "Crack!" of AKs always wakes me up because it's always incoming. It didn't last long. The "Pop! Pop! Pop!" of M-16s backed by cross-firing M-60 machineguns soon hogged the moonlight serenade. They were accompanied by the "Bloop-Blam!" antiphony of M-79 grenade launchers and the booming kettle-drum explosions of hand grenades.

I stayed rolled up tight during the brief exchange, one of the few bonuses of not carrying a weapon. Unless the conductor calls for "Medic," I don't budge. I know my cue. Every musician in this concerto of pain knew his part. In less than five minutes, the orchestra had ended; their audience was dead.

My solo came early the next morning as refugees from the all-night carnage of artillery began to come our way. I only remember one adult, a woman wounded in the side of the neck. I bandaged it, and then carried her to the helicopter.

"You know, Doc," said one Blue who had observed us, "you're a pretty good guy."

I smiled and nodded my thanks, but thought, 'Since when does that count for anything over here?'

We evacuated another 250 villagers, but it was the children that were the worst. They came to me with their arms held away from the sides of their bodies like baby chicks burned from the heat of exploding ordinances. Most had 2nd degree burns from the blasts. I used dry sterile dressings when and where I could, and treated about 30 of them. Then one little girl, all alone, broke my heart.

I saw her walking toward us through the sand from a hundred feet away. She couldn't have been much older than four or five herself, carrying a bundle half her size: her baby brother.

I took him from her immediately when I saw that he was bleeding from the forehead. She didn't protest.

A standard full-sized dressing would never do, but I had just the thing. While reconning the Med Supply tent, without Sgt. T-Rex,

I happened upon some miniature field dressings. I managed to scoop up just enough to give the appearance that they hadn't been touched.

Another Blue held the baby while I worked. After opening the waxed-paper and plastic layers of wrapping, I placed the dressing over the wound, and then secured the four ties around his head.

As I worked, the baby would cry some, then stop and just stare wide-eyed at nothing, then close its eyes and cry some more, before repeating the process.

The size and position of the baby bandage were perfect and I felt pleased. Then, as I was handing my pint-sized patient back to his sister, the baby went limp in my hands. He had lost too much of the little supply of blood he had. Infant or mistaken infantryman, he was dead.

His sister must have instinctively known he was gone and protested in her child's Vietnamese as I handed him back to her care. At the time, I didn't know what else to do.

Later, I wished I had just found an ammo box, emptied its lethal contents into the sand and replaced them with the tiny, sad corpse. Then I would have dug a small grave in the sand—with the muzzle of the nearest M-16 if I had to—and given him a proper burial. But if wars stopped to honor every innocent life lost, they'd never end . . . they never do anyway.

While evacuating villagers near a huge hay stack, someone opened up on us. As I belly-flopped into the sand, I considered the irony of it all. Here I was, skinny as a needle and trying to hide behind a haystack, while some peasant-farmer-turned-guerrilla rakes that same stack of hay with a "borrowed tool"—a Russian-designed, Chinese-made AK-47. 'This is nuts! Why are you shooting at me, Mo, you Commie Stooge?! I'm just here to help!'

Following the sniper's untimely passing, I decided I didn't want to die alone that day. So, after I treated the last villager and we evacuated them, I looked for Marty.

"Busy day, Doc?"

"Too busy, Marty, but it looks like it's near closing time." That's when a sniper opened up from the tree line across the rice paddy field. I had spoken too soon.

Marty and I dropped, saw a shell hole, and rolled into it. "Now this is what I call living!" I said. "Our own pre-fab foxhole!"

No sooner had we settled in, then an M-48 tank sweeping through the village toward us cut loose with its 90mm cannon—right over our heads. "Vaboom!" You'd think the world had ended.

"Marty, we've got to get out of this hole!" We exploded out of our sand trap like Jack Nicholas and ran as fast and as far away from that rolling fortress as possible. Where's a good RPG-7 when you need one?

By now, the gunships had chalked up the sniper and the battle was over. C Troop came through clean, except for Squirrel and the Fat FO; but the other Cav units had paid heavily: 4 KIA and 15 WIA, plus the 1/69th Armor's 8 KIAs I witnessed. Enemy losses were tallied at some 100 KIA.

One NVA who made it out was lying wounded in the sand. I ran over and was bandaging him up when a helicopter landed nearby. It was some Cav General—he could have been the Commanding General for all I knew, we didn't exactly run in the same circles. Soon, I could feel him breathing down my neck.

"Do you know what you're doing, Soldier?" he asked.

"Yes, Sir," I said.

"If you could pull him through it would be worth a million dollars to us, a million dollars!"

"Yes, Sir. Will do," I said, but I thought, 'General, just make that million-dollar check out to CFC Brad L. Smith—Civilian First Class.' "

As far as I know, the patient lived, but my imaginary check never cleared.

"Yes, Sir. Will do." That's how you talk to a General. When I was at the 67th Evac, General Westmoreland—at that time the Commanding General for the entire war—came by on a personal inspection tour. I stayed out of his way; I knew he couldn't send me anywhere worse than Vietnam, but he might send me somewhere colder, like the Aleutians.

Lacking discernment, a friend of mine ran into him head on. Westmoreland asked the Private what he could do for him. "Well, General," my friend replied, "we've got a sandbag detail over here if you'd like to lend a hand." Westmoreland just looked at him.

That's how *NOT* to talk to a General!

Chapter 42: Miscellaneous Mayhem

Some things you just don't write home about. For various reasons, they're better left unshared, especially with family. Still, they haunt me. How strange war can be, how sad, how insane. Case in point . . .

We were making our way down a sparsely wooded slope when I heard M-16s popping away from the squad behind. After picking myself up off the jungle floor, I ran back to see if I was needed. I wasn't.

A lone VC lay dead, face up, his chest a magnet full of .223 rounds. His only weapon was a U.S. grenade strapped to the front of his pistol belt . . . with dozens of rubber bands! Evidently, he was a Cong Kamikaze. He was supposed to run up, pull the pin, and dive into our formation, taking as many of us with him as possible. He was at least 20 yards away when our guys nailed him. Twenty yards is five yards beyond the effective shrapnel range of any grenade. Even if he had somehow succeeded and dived face first into our ranks, his own body would have absorbed most of the explosion.

Later, we speculated at how bad a Commie soldier you must have to be to be assigned to a suicide mission. We're talking low man on the dumb squad here. What a waste of a life.

The VC/NVA preferred our grenades because their ChiCom versions weren't very effective. One time, C Troop went up against some VC who had staked out their own private boulder fortress. From their 50-foot high lair, they began chucking ChiComs down at us. I was on the other side of the rock formation with another squad and the interpreter, Tong. We weren't in the line of fire, though I kept low anyway. We heard explosion after explosion, but were out of position to be of any help. I feared the worst, but every time we made radio contact with the squads under attack, they said they were all right, no problem. The grenades were either falling short or exploding with little more effect than a good-sized firecracker.

Even more bizarre was the fact that Tong sat on a rock, fully exposed to possible hostile fire, reading a book during the whole firefight. I pleaded with him to find cover, but he just ignored me and kept right on turning the pages of his paperback.

Eventually, the fortress VC either ran out of grenades or ran out of patience. Either way, they stopped throwing and we simply left the vicinity.

Maybe they took the "A" Tunnel home.

One of my first field casualties, prior to December 1st, was a punji stake wound—two wounds actually, one patient, one stake. The Pointman had walked into the stake hidden in some tall grass with his left foot. He then stepped back and stepped into it again with his right food. Now, punji stakes are sharpened bamboo blades covered with VC fecal matter . . . you might say they're a byproduct of war. Nasty. I treated the two puncture wounds with everything I had: Hydrogen Peroxide, Merthiolate, and Bacitracin. Because we were deep in the Boonies, we couldn't evac him out immediately.

"Here's a good place for a PZ (Pick-up Zone)," he'd say from time to time, but we had to keep moving—for the next two hours.

A couple of weeks later, I talked to several of the Blues back from the hospital. They told me that the doctors had just decided the day before NOT to amputate both the Pointman's legs!

Punji stakes are no picnic in the woods.

Punji Stake Pit protecting one of the Cu Chi Tunnels.

Another time we were going through a village. As I rounded a corner, I came face to face with something right out of a horror movie: a woman with no eyelids and a face full of scar tissue! Through the interpreter, I found out that as a child she had been horribly scalded from an accident with a cauldron of boiling rice water.

"We were the first ones here, Doc," said one of the guys. "You should have seen us jump!"

Sounds like Snow White's eighth dwarf: Jumpy.

One grunt from another unit I knew in the hospital told me of a bizarre encounter he had one night. He spotted the silhouette of a single figure which he took to be a VC guerrilla coming up the trail. He emptied a magazine into him from a good distance.

The next morning, he and his buddies found the corpse of a real gorilla lying dead there.

Guerrilla. Gorilla. At least they sound similar.

175

Another G.I. said that they were hunting elephants below the DMZ with their chopper's 40mm automatic grenade launchers. The Brass ordered them to waste the great animals because the VC/NVA were using them to carry mortar rounds and tubes.

Sorry, Dumbo, the 1st Air Cav is not that kind of flying circus.

Finally, I left my mark on Vietnam for posterity the last time I was in An Khe. As I made my way back to the barracks, at night and through unfamiliar territory, I wandered onto a construction site. Two steps later and I was boot deep in freshly poured cement.

I still imagine Victor Charlie viewing my version of Grauman's Chinese Theater, laughing, and then wondering what lame American made those prints.

Sorry, Charlie, no autographs.

Chapter 43: They Got Weise!

Pvt. Weise—pronounced "Wise," though most everyone mispronounced it "Weece"—embodied the nice, amiable, easy-going kind of guy who should never have been in combat. Again, nice is the operative word here; too nice for war. Yet, if Jimmy Stewart can fly 20 missions in a B-24 over Europe during World War II, who am I to judge?

Still, if they picked soldiers the way they pick grade-school players for dodge ball, I'd still take the fat kid on the end before Weise.

Weise was good for laughs, though. He always had a smile for you, like he really wasn't there in the worst war imaginable, but just dropped by to say, "Hi, guys! What's up? What do you want to do today? I'm game for about anything." Even carrying 40 pounds of radio on his back didn't seem to faze him.

He had a running joke that always broke us up. When a stray shot went off and we all hit the deck, we'd hear this frenzied voice say, "They got Weece!" It was Weise's voice.

The last day I ever saw him was on my last mission, a day we didn't even make it into combat.

I felt more tired than usual as I wedged myself and my aid bags into the chopper that morning. The night before, the Crew Chief/Door Gunner for Warrant Officer Hazelwood's helicopter woke me up at about 2:30. It was July 9.

"I can hardly breathe, Doc. It feels like somebody's sittin' on my chest."

There really wasn't anything I could do for his anxiety; my talents and training were limited. I used to tell guys like him, "Sorry, that's out of my league. Go get yourself shot first, and then I'll see what I can do for you."

But I didn't tell the Crew Chief that, he was too short—74 days and a wakeup. We all knew that most of us got it either in the first month of our tours or the last month. I could tell he was really stressed, so I just stayed up and talked with him for a while. Eventually, he calmed down enough so we could both go back to sleep.

I knew I'd be going back to Japan and then home anytime now, so the helicopter ride was almost enjoyable. The hundred-mile-per-hour wind racing past just two feet from our faces was the closest thing we had to air conditioning. And the view was other worldly. Maybe I'd retire here someday, after the war was won.

Hydraulics failure caused the first chopper to go down from 500 feet. Warrant Officer John Hazelwood was the pilot, a pro, but the bird still hit hard enough to injure everyone in third squad.

The second squad chopper was the real problem. When its pilot saw the first slick in trouble, he made a drastic dive to get to it, so drastic that he almost collided with one of our gunships flying below. In an erratic maneuver to avoid a mid-air crash, he lost power.

From above, we could see the crippled chopper in a slow-motion ballet of humanity and insanity, twisting, pointing straight down at times, and turning. The tail rotor must have sustained damage or even breakage. It was out of sync with the main rotor, causing the whole craft to rotate wildly underneath.

Everywhere you look: Rice Paddies!

Finally, the stricken slick plowed into the rain-swollen rice paddies. As it turned on its side, the huge spinning blades impacted the paddy dikes at 9,000 rpm, exploding into dozens of lethal lances. Then the craft just lay there like some great, fallen dinosaur.

As soon as we touched down, I was out the door running to the first chopper. I tried to cut across one paddy, but the combined goo of water, mud, buffalo manure, and human waste forced me to turn around. I ran along the perimeter of the dikes instead.

One of the pilots was lying on a paddy dike laughing. The co-pilot was with him.

"Don't mind me, Doc," he said. "I'm all right. Help the others." Then he laughed some more. I suspected he was hurt far worse than he knew; possibly a broken back.

"Don't move him until I come back," I yelled as I ran by. "And don't let him get up."

By the time I reached the second squad chopper, still on its side and venting fuel into the paddy, most of the walking wounded were already on gunships ready to be airlifted out. I joined another trooper on the skid of the downed chopper, a neat trick since it was sticking up in the air above us. Together we peered into the open chasm that had been the left doorway of the machine.

"Weise is still down there," he said.

There was no "They got Weise!" this time. This time it was for real. This time it wasn't funny.

"He's pinned under the fuselage. We can't get to him. They've got a Chinook coming."

The twin-propped, Greyhound bus-sized Chinook would hook onto the smaller Huey D and lift it off Weise. At least, that was the plan.

"Are you OK?" I called.

"I think so, Doc, but I can't move."

That could mean anything. "Hold on. We'll get you out of there in no time."

The lumbering sky pickup truck looked like an angel when it finally arrived. The crew attached cables and then directed the pilot as he lifted the downed slick straight up. We could see Weise now on his back, and everything looked good—until the Chinook drug the Huey's tail along the ground and right across Weise's body!

As one, our hearts and breathing stopped. Seeing a friend die in combat is one thing. Watching him killed by Government-

Issued incompetence is another. How could anyone have survived that?

Pancaked into the South Asian landscape, more rice paddy than person, Weise's smile shown through the mud. When I saw that he was alive, I visibly began to sob from relief.

"It's OK, Doc," he said weakly. "I'm all right."

He was trying to comfort me! I got myself back under control. If the sunglasses I always wore weren't able to mask my feelings anymore, maybe it was time to go home—past time.

After checking Weise for bleeding and broken bones—neither of which he had—we carefully loaded him onto a stretcher and gunshipped him out.

That's when I noticed several guys huddled together. They were looking at something buried in the mud: a body!

You could barely see his back sticking up out of the paddy quagmire. When the chopper rolled on its side, he must have been thrown clear, only to have the vacant machine gun mount hit him in the back and plunge him face down into the suffocating mud, burying him alive.

When we turned the body over, I recognized him from the night before: it was the Crew Chief.

I've always wondered if his breathlessness in the AM hours wasn't some kind of premonition about how he would die the next day. The thought still haunts me. I hope he was out cold or already dead when it happened. I hope he didn't suffer.

July 10

The day before yesterday, I waded in the South China Sea—aid bags and all. We were sweeping a village along the coast and set up our PZ on the beach.

I should be on my way to Qui Nhon tomorrow or the next day. Most likely they'll operate again on my arm and evacuate me out to Japan.

See if you can get hold of the June issue of Popular Mechanics. *It has an article on the Viet Cong weapons in it. Of the five it has illustrated, I've been shot at by every kind at least once. I've carried three of them, too.*

Love, Brad

Chapter 44: Going Home

That was my last letter from the field. I left Two Bits and C Troop that day. Sgt. Sam gave me the news,

"You've got 15 minutes to collect your gear and make it out on the next chopper, Doc. You're going home." We both understood I would be in an Army hospital in Japan for months before, but it didn't matter.

I stood there stunned. War today, home tomorrow. At least I'd be able to say goodbye to Marty and the other guys at the 67 Evac Hospital.

Then he added, "Thanks for being there for the Troop, Doc."

"Thank you, Sgt. Sam," I said, "for helping keep me alive."

Earlier, another sergeant—the big guy with the Fu Manchu mustache who had carried the wounded NVA lifer out like a baby—said I was the best Medic C Troop ever had. That one turned me red, I was just doing my job. "Hero" was a four-letter word to all of us. We were all just doing our jobs.

At the 67th Evac Hospital, I found Marty and eight of our guys in one ward. They were clean, shaven, and wearing light blue pajamas. They looked like some demented college preppie party.

Marty had a badly cut and swollen lip. Every time I said something funny, he'd wince. Smiling hurt him. "No, don't make me laugh," he'd say in a muffled voice. "It hurts too much." Then I'd say something again, and he'd hold his face and roll over on one side.

The trooper with the bullet hole through the Confederate flag on his helmet said he lost his helmet in the crash.

Another Blue had his helmet crushed. The helicopter had come down on it, with his head still inside, and squeezed him out like toothpaste from a tube. His whole head was one big swollen mass of hematoma.

"Look at this, Doc," he said. Then he pushed his thumb into the side of his face and left an inch-deep impression. It didn't fill up for several minutes.

"Wow," I said. "Nice trick." What else could I say?

I still had my own helmet with me, even though I had changed to a fatigue cap. I shoved the helmet under one of the hospital cots. Why I didn't just stuff it into my duffel bag and take it home for a souvenir, I'll never know. It had the portrait of

"Angelique," a fantasy girl that Marty drew for me on the camouflage cover. Marty was an artist and it was a work of art. Funny how much she looked like my future wife, Donna, who I wouldn't meet for another three years.

Saying goodbye at the hospital made my departure special. That's the image of my guys at C Troop that I still carry with me: happy, laughing, clean, safe.

They flew me out to the 249th Hospital outside of Tokyo, Japan. I underwent extensive surgery on my arm, an ulna nerve transposition. The doctors told me they would never have even tried it 10 years before. For another month and a half, I underwent physical therapy, but since nerve tissue only regenerates at the rate of one inch a month, it would take 18 months for it to recover. It never did recover 100 percent.

At Thanksgiving, 15 years later, I visited the Vietnam Wall, two weeks after it opened to the public. I drove there from my in-laws' home in York, Pennsylvania, alone, before daybreak. That's the way I wanted it.

In the best traditions of my high school nickname, Wrong-Way Smith, I got lost coming into Washington, D.C. I drove around until I turned onto one particularly wide boulevard. 'Nice neighborhood,' I thought. A block later, I drove past the White House!

I parked on the Washington Monument-side of the mall and began walking. As I closed in on the Lincoln Memorial at the other end, still not having found the Vietnam Memorial, I noticed a stand of blood-red trees to my right. Their fall brilliance took my breath away. Then I looked below the knoll where they stood and saw a black slash in the green hillside: The Wall.

For a long time, I stood off at a distance, taking it all in. I was afraid to go any closer, afraid of the names I might find there. I hadn't come to look up the names of those friends I knew were there, but rather to look up the names of those guys I left in the 67th Evac ward, to see if they'd made it back or not.

Even in the crisp fall air, I could feel my palms sweat as I thumbed through the Vietnam Wall phone book that listed names alphabetically for a wall where names were listed chronologically. It was a thick phone book.

Slowly, painfully, I checked each row and each line, hoping for the best; fearing the worst. None of my friends' names were in the "dead" numbers book or etched on that black marble. Thank You, Lord!

Return to Vietnam 1995
Some of the Old Guard of the 25th Infantry Division paying their respects at an NVA "Heroes" graveyard? Or were they simply checking the dates to see if they might have contributed to their ranks!

After my leave, I was assigned to the Letterman General Army Hospital at the Presidio, San Francisco, just five hundred miles from home. I was up for Specialist 5, when I discovered that none of my Vietnam medals, including my Purple Heart and Air Medal, were in my records. I spoke to my CO, Colonel Lesser. Like a character pulled from Heller's *Catch 22*, he had just been promoted from—that's right—Major Lesser. As a captain, Lesser had been shot through the side after leaving his downed chopper to attack an enemy position on foot! He pulled his rank and was able to get me those decorations. Actually, though, with 110 combat assaults by helicopter, I had earned four decorations of the Air

Medal. I didn't say anything about a possible Bronze Star Medal at the time because I was still in that Nam "hero-is-a-four-letter-word" mindset. Besides, at the time, I had heard about it from just one C Troop Crew Chief who I had only just met.

Twenty-five years later, however, I happened to call ex-trooper Rowdy in Fort Wayne, Indiana. After Vietnam, he became a mail carrier. He told me Sgt. Sam had put all three of us—Rowdy, Martinez, and me—in for the Silver Star for what we did for Sgt. Cain on December 1st. Then he said the Silver Star had been downgraded to a Bronze Star Medal because Sgt. Samuel and Sgt. Haskett had received the Silver Star, and Sgt. Kaneshiro was awarded the Distinguished Service Cross; all for their actions on December 1st. Later, I found out that a number of the records for the 1st Cav for 1967-1968 had been destroyed in a fire, too. For whatever the reason, I never did receive the Bronze Star Medal. Neither did Rowdy or Martinez.

I petitioned the Army Medals Board for my medal. For credibility, I included a full account of the incident and affidavits from both Rowdy and Matt. Matt had been there when General SLAM Marshall had flown in and presented several of us, including me, with an impact Bronze Star Medal. Except I wasn't there at the time, I was still recovering in the hospital at Camp Zama, Japan.

In essence, the bureaucrats on the Board told me I had waited too long to submit my request. They also cast veiled doubts on the credibility of my friends, even though Rowdy was a career civil servant, and Matt (Matthew Brennan) had written and published several best-sellers on the 1/9th Cav in Vietnam. Matt had returned to Nam for another tour, three all tolled!

Rowdy also told me that C Troop changed after I left, though it had nothing to do with me; it was never about me.

He related how three months later, the NVA set a trap for the 1/9th. They moved in 12.7mm anti-aircraft machine guns and 37mm cannons, lots of them. Then they let some of their personnel be seen from the air and waited.

When the first of our choppers came to investigate, they shot them down. They shot down those choppers with their crews and the troops they carried. They shot them right out of the skies like clay pigeons at a skeet match. Then they waited a while for the next flight and shot them down, too.

Some of them made it back. Rowdy said he witnessed one chopper that reached the airfield, just before it blew up overhead. In all, the 1/9th lost 28 out of the 29 helicopters it sent out that day! It was the Little Big Horn all over again for the 1st Cav.

I've never seen this incident recorded in any 1st Cav or Army histories. Nor have I seen these kinds of losses tabulated. But if Rowdy, who was there, says he saw it happen, it happened.

I arranged to see Rowdy again after 25 years when I was passing through Fort Wayne, Indiana. Once in town, however, I was unable to reach him by phone.

A month later, after returning home from my trip, I received a letter. It was from Rowdy's wife. She said he had really enjoyed talking to me on the phone. When he hung up, however, and went to bed that night, he had a nightmare. It was about the war, the same bad dream Rowdy always had.

His wife said he had it every time he saw something about the war on TV, read about Vietnam, talked to someone about it, or even just thought too long on what happened over there. And he had this nightmare every night for a month!

After the debacle in the fall of 1967, new tactics and better equipment were needed fast. Pink Teams were born: White scout and Red gunships working in tandem. The last time I was in An Khe, I saw one of these future team members: the first Cayuse scout helicopter delivered to the Cav. You couldn't tell how fast, maneuverable, and well-armed it was by looking at it. The craft was on static display only, high on a pedestal, and well within the interior of the compound for safe keeping.

The other half of the killing equation was the Cobra, the first chopper designed and built exclusively as an attack helicopter, the forerunner of today's Apache.

The Cayuse would fly low as bait, until it drew fire. Then the Cobra would strike with mini-guns and rockets. Pretty in Pink they were not.

During Operation Pershing, from February 1967 to January 1968, before the Tet Offensive, the 88 helicopters of the 1/9th Cav were replaced twice over. Fourteen were shot down and another 105 were shot up so badly that they had to be scrapped.

For the 770 men of the 1/9th Cav in 1967, the statistics were even more sobering: 55 KIA, 1 MIA, and 264 WIA. That's a casualty rate of 42 percent! Those are the kind of numbers you don't want to know before you join a unit or while you're with it. Ignorance is bliss.

Vietnam War Women's Memorial.

Over the ten months I was overseas, I spent three months recuperating—a month and a half at Camp Zama Hospital and a month and a half at Camp Drake's 249th Army Hospital. Then I spent two more months assigned to the 67th Evac in Qui Nhon trying to get back to C Troop while I built barracks, stacked weapons, and held mail call. So, just five months of my tour was actually spent in combat.

But during those five months, I made more than 110 combat assaults by helicopter and was actively involved in 13 firefights. Thirteen firefights over a five-month span of time averages out to about one every other week. The typical average for non-airmobile outfits in Vietnam was two firefights PER YEAR. We saw that much combat in a single MONTH with the 1/9th. Helicopters got you there faster and more often, multiplying your chances of finding and fighting the enemy. This was especially true if you were Recon. Non-airmobile outfits may have gone in by chopper, but then they spent days and even weeks plodding through the jungles before being picked up again. C Troop often made two, three, or even four LZs a day! If we didn't find anything the first time, our slicks picked

us up and flew us to another area of suspected enemy movement .
. . then another . . . and another. This might explain our 42 percent
casualty rate in 1967, more than double that of the rest of the 1st
Cav Division, and six times the figure for a regular infantry outfit in
Vietnam. So, if you were seriously gun shy, the 1/9th Cav and C
Troop were not for you.

Besides being shot at all those times—including being
strafed by one of our own gunships—I had a 175mm artillery round
drop close enough to knock me off my feet, even though it didn't
explode. (Question: What do you get when an artillery shell scores
a direct hit on a Doc named Smith? Answer: Smithereens.) An M-
48 tank fired its 90mm gun over my head at nearly point-blank
range. I was also a passenger on a flight of four helicopters when
two of them crashed, and I was on one of the two choppers that
didn't crash.

Another helicopter I rode on blew out something vital through
the side of its engine compartment right next to me. I saw it go
flying out of the side of the craft like ozone through the
stratosphere. We had to limp back to base, just barely making it.

Yet another "chopper" lived up to its nickname by lopping off
the top of a five-inch diameter tree while it was flying us out of a PZ.
The diameter at which the tree wins and the blade loses is reported
to be six inches.

In the tall grass at one hot LZ, I nearly sat on a punji stake.
Another time, I grabbed the business end of a giant crossbow. I
also fell through a paddy dike up to my armpits, with the rest of my
body hanging inside a VC tunnel.

Yet, the worst way I almost died had nothing to do with the
enemy or the mechanisms of death. It was purely natural, even
organic.

We were searching yet another village—slow, tedious work
with more stops and delays than Amtrak. At the time, I prided
myself for my quick reaction time and ability to know where to go
when the going got hot.

As we waited for something to be checked out ahead, I
noticed a picturesque little ravine tucked between the villages, just
beyond the last group of hooches. It was about 30 feet long and 5
feet deep, with gently sloping sides covered with grass.

'Now, that's where I'm going if we get shot at,' I thought. 'In fact, why don't I just jump into it right now and try it on for size.'

I was moving to do just that when we got the order to move out. As we walked along the path that paralleled my little lost sanctuary, I noticed that its grassy sides were moving. In fact, they were slithering! Pit Vipers! Scores of snakes filled every foot of that ravine from end to end.

I visibly shivered at how close I'd come to a gruesome death. Even if I had somehow survived the initial 20 or 30 bites, there would have been no way any of the Blues could have gotten me out of there. All they would have been able to do is mercifully put me out of my misery:

"Would someone please shoot the Doc, quick? He's gone and gotten himself killed. Alabama? Hunter? Do we have time to fly in Sgt. T-Rex?"

We may have been the killingest troop (C Troop) of the killingest unit (1st Squadron/9th Cavalry Brigade) of the killingest division (1st Cavalry Division Airmobile) of the Vietnam War in 1967, but we paid a terrible price to be number one. Many of us, like Rowdy, are still paying our dues . . . long after the In-Country Club has disbanded. I'm paying mine right now just writing this book.

Vietnam was supposed to be my Olympics. I trained for it, dreamed about it, sacrificed for it. The U.S. was supposed to win and I was destined to medal. But it didn't and neither did I. I earned the Air Medal—actually four awards for more than 100 combat assaults by helicopter, though I only received the first one. And I received the Purple Heart, of course, but nothing for valor.

I had neuroma—nerve tissue clogging the passage of impulses through the ulna nerve to the muscles of my hand. They surgically removed the bad growth, moved the nerve—the "Funny Bone"—from its God-willed position on the exterior of my arm, over and around the elbow, to its new Man-made place at the interior of my arm.

After my third operation, my five-inch long scar was intersected with another thirteen-inch scar, running the length of my arm from the wrist, past the elbow, and along the triceps. Together, the two scars form an almost perfect cross. I have a feeling I'll be able to take that one with me . . . not like a Silver Star or a Bronze Star Medal left molding in a box in the attic.

Receiving the Purple Heart from Gen. Jingles at the Presidio, San Francisco.

The last dog I'll ever own was named Suzie. We rescued her from a local shelter. She was two years old, and marked to be put down, when my five-year-old daughter said, "Daddy, I really want this one." Christine was in the minority; Suzie had been abandoned three times by two different owners.

In the eleven years Suzie lived with us, she became family. She and I walked together more than 3,000 miles. I lost 50 pounds with her by my side, so in a way, Suzie helped save my life, too.

When she became ill with cancer and the vet put her down, California law forbid burying her in our backyard, so I imagined the pros at the animal hospital would take care of the body. They did.

Later, I found out that Suzie had most likely been tossed into a plastic garbage bag with a dozen other euthanized pets and dumped into the bottom of a landfill.

That's what it felt like coming home from Vietnam!

We were bagged and buried, without ceremony, discarded and forgotten. It didn't matter how many miles we had walked or how many lives we had saved. We just became part of a landfill for a new housing project, just like the graves of those Vietnamese in Bong Son had become landfill for LZ Two Bits.

Burying the past under the future never makes for a better tomorrow. It only makes for a tolerable today.

Chapter 45: Collateral Damage

There's one last incident I'd like to share. It was the first thing I ever published about the war. It appeared in *Today's Christian Woman* magazine in the fall of 1978. I think it sums up the whole experience; not just my experience, but all of ours. For that reason, I wrote it in the third person narrative. I call it:

People, Promises, and Other Broken Things

The young Medic stood stoop-shouldered beneath his pressing yoke of two decades of life. The last six months had bent and wasted him the most, six months spent treading water in the whirlpool of war, in the cesspool of Vietnam.

Now it was spring and the boy climbed a hill alone. Treks like this one would age him the most. The sergeant said, "The Fighter Red gunship just killed a pregnant woman. Go on up the hill and see what you can do for the baby."

The Medic looked out from the narrow world beneath his helmet. If his face showed some signs of expressing his emotions, his eyes didn't, they never did. That's what the dark glasses were for—not to shield him from the sun—but to conceal his fear, his sadness, his shame. Windows to the soul needed to be shut tight in a war.

Head down, his hands and forearms resting on the twin medical aid bags belted about his hips, he trudged upwards. Heat in the hundreds, humidity close behind, the youth's steel helmet and rightly termed "fatigues" acted like a pressure cooker. Sweat saturated his close-cropped hair and rolled out of every pore in his skinny body, soaking his ill-fitting, clownish costume.

All these things seemed incidental now, where moments before they monopolized his thoughts. Now the youth burned with the intense realization that his private war—and maybe his personal Hell—awaited him just over the next ridge . . . .

The woman lay still, her face forever contorted in that final expression of agony. Her stomach was bared and swelling from her body like some extinct volcano, never to erupt the life it contained.

She might have been Mary with mankind's long-awaited promise of salvation lying still and lifeless within her, a prenatal victim of satanic cunning. She might have been, but instead she was just another forgotten fling of some faceless, nameless Robin Hood, or more likely, the pass-around rose of all the Merry Men; the girl who made the team.

For long, somber moments he stared at her. Lying face up upon the hillside with her round stomach and breasts, she seemed to blend in with the undulating countryside. It was as if she and the betrayed promise of new beginnings inside her were one with the land, inseparable, indistinguishable from Vietnam itself.

Many years later, when the war and South Vietnam had finally and disgracefully been lost, the pieces of the young Medic that survived and found their place in the puzzle of manhood thought again of this incident. Only then did he realize that all of Vietnam—North and South—was that dead pregnant woman on the hill. The Communists had whispered sweet lies of undying love in one ear, while they used her for their own selfish ends. When the embryo of a new, better life began to take shape within her, she was abandoned to the ravages of war. Dying, the promise died with her, never to be realized.

But she listened to us with the other ear, and we fathered those bastard promises within her, too. We left her unloved, unwed, and pregnant, and then deserted them both—mother and child—to die on a distant and lonely mountainside.

"See what you can do for the baby . . . ." The hopelessness of those words hit home with increasing irony, until they seemed almost laughable.

Back down the hill, the Medic thought of what he would say to those who waited. He knew these old-young men he walked death's narrow causeway with were long since divorced from any natural feelings. They willed to know only steel—steel from them, steel around them, and with some, steel within them. It is the steel that weighs heaviest on a man who has touched war, and in turn, been touched—and must bear the imprint of war's gauntlet for the rest of his life.

No, the Medic would play their game, too, if he wanted to survive the war of nerves.

"Seven pounds, eight ounces—a boy," reported the Medic. "I'm naming him Fighter Red."

The muffled echo of hollow laughter rose and died quickly— a roar only heard amid the mocking lions and still-born promises of a lost war.

Epilogue

China Beach from the bluffs above.

The 1st Cavalry Division Airmobile constituted a unique unit for a unique—though brief—time. The Cavalry division that traded horses for tanks in one war, now traded its tanks for helicopters; swapping heavy ground armor for aluminum sky choppers.

In 1965, the new 1st Cavalry Division Airmobile, the 1st Air Cav, swooped from the sky and touched down on Vietnam soil. During the course of the war, the "First Team" proved to be just that—winning Olympic-class warriors with a game plan that decimated VC and NVA enemy forces wherever it roamed.

In 1971, the 1st Air Cav left South Vietnam. By 1975, the "Airmobile" had been dropped from its name and the division changed back into just another armored outfit.

For me, that will always be like wrapping an eagle in layers of lead foil, to watch it slowly writhe and die.

In the spring of 1975, I watched the fall of Saigon on TV . . . or at least I tried to watch it. It's hard when you're hanging your head. I wept for the thousands of Vietnamese civilians pressing up against the U.S. Embassy's high iron gates like so much cheese through a grater. The Marine guards treated them like they were past their expiration date. Then the Navy pushed our Huey helicopters off its overcrowded carrier decks and let them sink into the South China Sea, and something sunk in me. Peace with Honor? Not where I sat. We did not finish well.

Saigon used to be *A Tale of Two Cities*, known as both "The Jewel of the Orient" and "The Whore City." So, I guess it was only fitting when the Communists—Victor Charlie—renamed it "Ho's City." Both the city and the victors belong in a Red Light district.

I have my mom to thank for saving the letters I wrote home, some three dozen which are included in this book. I say that I have Mom to thank because I noticed Dad had written notes on the back of some of the envelopes, reminders to pick up this or that at the hardware store or pay an insurance bill. Mom retrieved and pasted the letters in a scrapbook, one with a big, yellow 1st Cav patch glued to the cover. Thanks, Mom! And it's OK, Dad; it wasn't your war.

My dad's war was the big one: World War II. It was Mom's war, too, of course; it was everyone's war back then, nothing like Nam. While Mom waited and prayed for his safe return, she worked in defense plants across Indiana, making bombers and fighters. When she left, they had to replace her with two male workers.

My dad was a hard worker, too, but he preferred to work smarter. He was a lot smarter than I was, anyway. His mom had instilled in him a life-long love for cooking, before she died when he was ten and he was shuffled off to live with a half-brother and his family. Those skills in the kitchen kept him out of combat. He was so good, in fact, that for a time he cooked just for the officers.

He did have one close call, though. After a safe and respectable time following D-Day, his unit landed in France. A Tech Sergeant by then, my dad was in charge of a number of other cooks.

Early one morning, they were all sleeping in one end of their mobile kitchen, when something exploded in the section containing the stoves. It was almost dawn.

"One of you men," said my sergeant/dad, "left a pot on the stove, and now we've got a mess to clean up—besides making breakfast! Get up. Let's get going."

I remember my dad smiling as he related how he opened the kitchen door to find shafts of the first morning's light streaming through holes in the ceiling. A Messerschmitt 109 fighter had strafed their column! My dad managed to sleep through his only combat.

Maybe "only" combat is a bit misleading. After VJ-Day, coming home on the Queen Mary, temporarily converted into a troop ship, Dad broke wind lying on the top bunk. And in a "Take No Prisoners" effort still studied in military circles today, he single-handedly cleared out the personnel in the four bunks below.

Perhaps, though, his best battle was his last—below decks and with a deck—when he liberated $900 from the liberators of Europe in a poker game.

When Dad got home, he packed up Mom and his cooking talent and moved to California. Starting as a short-order cook chopping lettuce, he rose through the ranks to chef, head chef, manager, and eventually owner. He built a couple of restaurants, played golf, traveled, and then retired to Palm Desert.

Like I said, smarter.

The last thing I ever saw of my dad were his feet . . . sticking out from under a sheet . . . at the Eisenhower Medical Center. Even without his boots, they looked like a soldier's feet.

His heart had finally given out on the third time around: a heart attack at age 57, then 72, and finally at 74, a week before Father's Day. I had purchased him a whole CD collection of the Big Band sounds from World War II. Costco took it back, no questions asked.

My dad's high-arched, tread-bare feet had taken him across Europe—to victory; my feet had taken me across Southeast Asia—to considerably less. Yet, a sheet waited for both of us. Not much difference between a white-cotton sheet and an olive-drab poncho liner.

It's like they say, win or lose, at the end of the game the pieces all go back into the same box. Still, we both believed that death is just a Friday afternoon gone wrong . . . but Sunday morning is coming to set things right.

In February 1985, World Vision sent me on assignment to Sudan, Africa. I wrote stories and took photos of their relief efforts during the war in neighboring Chad. Some 23,000 refugees lived in shanties of cardboard boxes and plastic tarps at the ACROSS relief camp. It lay just six miles from the border.

The children suffered the most. Many of them were no more than living skeletons. So, I experienced yet another side of war: the underfed underbelly.

I was in Sudan for five weeks. I almost skipped to the plane I was so glad to leave that hot, dusty, horrible place. I looked forward to being home with my wife a good, long time.

Two months later, I was back in Africa—in an even worse place. World Vision had sent out a call for a journalist to go to Uganda. No one volunteered out of some 4,000 staff, except a 50-year-old manager. He had been a National Geographic editor, written an acclaimed book on his travels along the Nile, and had only just married and begun a family. When I spoke to him, I could tell he wasn't keen on going. Besides, he was too valuable to go. I wasn't and I knew it. Still expendable.

World Vision knew it, too. It put out another organization-wide request. I told my manager that if they didn't find anybody this time, I'd go. They didn't; I went.

The only reoccurring dream I had from the Vietnam War was that I was back in combat again, being asked to do the same things, but this time I was pushing 40. I always woke up before the dream played out. I never found out if I could still do it or not, if I still had what it takes.

Now, I had a new dream. I was climbing a wall. As I put my hands on the top of it to pull myself up and over, two gnarled, ugly hands covered mine. I thought, 'Whatever is on the other side won't be as bad as I imagine, it never is.' When I raised myself up to see whatever was there, I came face to face with the most horrible, hideous creature I'd ever seen—far worse, in fact, than I could ever have imagined. Then, I woke up.

Afraid for my life? Afraid of going back into a war zone? Is that what 20 years had done to me? Do the years really make cowards of us all? Even me, C Troop's Doc Smith? Medic Man?

I prayed about my fears, wringing out my soul through my eyes, night after night. Finally, it came to me: I wasn't afraid for myself, for my safety. I was afraid of what I would have to see again—that ghoul on the other side of the wall in my dream—the suffering and horror of war.

After that, I was all right; no more dreams. In fact, my attitude took a 180-degree turn. I told myself, 'Bring it on! I've been to war. I've seen it all. Nothing you've got will surprise me.'

I could not have been more wrong.

In Uganda, Idi Amin had been deposed; but his generals, especially Milton Obote, were even worse. Their Northern controlling faction butchered more than 500,000 people in the South.

In the three days we spent in the Luwero Triangle, known as the "Killing Fields" of the war, I counted more than 500 skulls in rows. The locals had brought them out so the world might see for itself the years of uncontrolled carnage. In the middle of one of those fields, I had to carefully pick my path so as not to step on human bones. We even found a rusty crank shaft among the scattered skeletons that had been used to crush the skulls of people when the sadists ran out of ammunition or grew bored with just shooting them.

But all this wasn't the monster of my subconscious.

'I wonder if I ever looked that young when I was in uniform.' I thought, as I observed the victorious rebel troops manning a checkpoint. I thought they couldn't have been much older than ten or twelve, but that was ridiculous. Ugandan men must just look younger.

The next afternoon I was driving with Kofee Hagen, the Interim Director of the fledgling World Vision program in Uganda. I was officially the Interim Communications Manager. Several rebel soldiers crossed the street ahead of us. Their AK-47s dwarfed them. Kofee noticed my shocked expression.

"They're Boy Soldiers," he said, to my unasked question.

"How old are they?"

"Probably eight or nine," he replied.

"Eight or nine?!"

"Many are only seven, some are even as young as five. Their parents were killed by the Northern government troops, often right in front of them. The boys and some girls escaped into the jungle. A few were so young that they lived with the monkeys and even forgot how to speak. The rebel troops found them, gave them an AK, and taught them how to use it. They didn't have to teach them how to hate.

"President Museveni used 300 of them as a spearhead when he attacked and took the capital of Kampala. He has half a dozen of them around him at all times as bodyguards, even now. Their loyalty to him is unquestioned."

So the world had found yet another way to revolve even lower in its downwardly spiraling orbit. Just when you think it couldn't, it does. Now it was arming the innocent and sending them off to war. I knew what that experience did to 19- and 20-year-old men. What must it do to five-year-old children?

The ghoul at the top of the wall *was* more horrible than I could have ever imagined. My dream was prophetic.

A week later, when Kofee asked me what area of need we should recommend to World Vision as the most urgent, it was an easy call. In the end, they established half a dozen programs for the orphaned Boy Soldiers, including one for their rehabilitation back into civilized society.

From 1988 to 2003, I worked for Mission Aviation Fellowship (MAF) as its Senior Staff Writer. Now this noteworthy organization can be described as "small planes, in faraway places, and pilots braver than their years." At least that's how I described it in one of our publications. For some 70 years, MAF has operated single-engine bush planes in Africa, Asia, Latin America, and Indonesia for the benefit of the people living there by supporting medical efforts, disaster relief, education, missionaries, and indigenous churches.

Ecuador 1998: Taking one of the MAF pilot's pet Boa Constrictors for a walk.

I traveled to their bases in Venezuela, Ecuador, and Mexico. For southern Mexico, I helped raise the funds, and bent my back a little, to build a simple church on a hillside in Oaxaca, a hotbed of spiritism. The 26-year-old itinerant pastor there had survived 14 attempts on his life—that's one more than I survived in Vietnam. Seems to me a man like that deserves a place to preach, even if the walls are adobe and the roof fashioned from sheets of corrugated zinc.

One of the execs at the MAF headquarters in Redlands, California (now in Boise, Idaho), asked me if I'd teach his son, David, how to spit shine his shoes before he entered West Point. After pulling out a tin of black Kiwi wax, filling the lid with water, and soaking a couple of cotton balls, I was ready. As we shined our low quarters together, I told him war stories—many of the same ones I'm telling you; except when we're through, you won't be able to see your reflection on the highly polished surface of your shoes.

Four years later, I was at a party to congratulate 2nd Lieutenant David upon his graduation, before he deployed to Iraq. He was standing with his brother when I walked up. He recognized me . . . or maybe it was my stories. I said, "The only advice I have for you is this: Remember, once you pull the pin, Mr. Grenade is not your friend."

A year later I heard that he'd received the Bronze Star Medal and later made Captain. I like to think the flash of his dress shoes had something to do with it.

In 1995, the year before my dad died of congestive heart failure, he paid my way to return to Vietnam with a dozen other vets. He knew what going back to Vietnam meant to me, even though Dad never said it in so many words. Heroes are like that.

We landed in Hanoi. Gary Barfoot, a retired Air Force Lt. Col. and a good friend of mine at MAF, had been a B-52 bomber pilot for two tours over the North. "Don't mention my name when you arrive there," he said. "Last time I was over there, the doors were open!"

Hanoi, 1995: Lively children play in front of the lethal legacy of Ho Chi Minh's tomb.

We visited the Ho Chi Minh mausoleum. Like Lenin in Red Square, Ho's remains had been preserved so that they could be viewed lying in state. A la Snow White, Ho reclined in a glass case, only this fairy tale came equipped with AK-47-wielding honor guards positioned at each corner. They were as coldly still as he was.

Ho's bald head and white-whiskered face blazed with reflected light. It reminded me of my four-year-old's Glo Worm doll. Ho the guerrilla leader; Ho the Communist revolutionary; Ho the night light.

No talking was allowed, period. When we exited and could breathe again, Hoot, a Paramedic and my roommate, showed us what he had hidden in his pocket: a tape recorder. He switched it on and played us a recording he had made of his buddies snoring at the fire house. Hoot had intended to play it as we passed Ho's crypt, but thought better of it when he saw the humorless guards. Good thing, too, or we might still be there.

"Uncle Ho," the children call him, an old man, dead for decades, still venerated by a people he led into slavery at the cost of millions of their lives and tens of thousands of ours.

No Moses was Ho.

We tried to attend church one Sunday in Da Nang. The Communists put the pastor on house arrest and directed us to start painting the local orphanage a day early. No, the Communists hadn't changed any; they never will.

I noticed many of my fellow vets were really bonding with the orphans and the Vietnamese people. They were very emotional. I wasn't. Then it hit me: they had been behind an M-16 or M-60 the last time they were here. The Vietnamese hadn't been people to them, they'd been collateral damage at best, targets at the worst. Now, they were relating to them one on one, as persons, as individuals.

I wasn't feeling much of anything, and I knew the reason for that, too. As a Medic, I had to suspend my emotions to treat horrific wounds caused by modern warfare. I separated the person from the body, regarding the latter as a spoiled piece of meat when I had to treat someone.

As a Journalist, the job I had been doing in and out of Africa and Latin America for the past 10 years, I had to feel the emotions of my subjects to write about them.

Back in Vietnam, I was stuck somewhere in between. As a Medic, I had to deny my emotions. As a Journalist, I had to rely on my emotions. So, as a result of the inner tug of war, I felt nothing. Zero. Nada. A draw.

Vietnam 1995: Return of The (Un)Original Thirteen
Hoot and Michael are second and third from the left. Second from the right is Retired Col. Dennis Stussie. Sixth from the right is Dave DeVries. I'm fourth from the right—Indiana Smith.

Several of the guys started the paperwork to adopt some of the Vietnamese kids. Eventually, four of them became Americans. Two teenage sisters, Thanh and Thuy, were adopted by former 25th Infantry Division sergeant Dave DeVries and his wife. He knew they would be turned out into the streets the next year. Today, they are Americans, happily married with families of their own.

Another MAF pilot friend of mine on the trip, Dennis Stussie, who had flown Mohawk counter-insurgency "Nighthawk" aircraft along the Ho Chi Minh Trail, organized the trip for International Aid. He invited me along for a reduced fare if I would take photos, something I did professionally for World Vision and Mission Aviation Fellowship.

His roommate, Floyd Olsen, from Wheaton College—where Todd Beamer of 9/11's Flight 93 had attended—had flown in Vietnam, too. His helicopter had been shot down and his body never recovered. We set out to find what we could about what happened to him. I was a Wheaton graduate, too.

204

Old soldiers on one last mission to find out the fate of a fallen friend.

We drove out to the area in question. Unlike the Vietnam I remembered, long strands of wire hung over rice paddies between the villages. They spoiled the scenery. I took them for some advancement in communication.

"They're communication wires, all right," our interpreter Michael told me, "so the Communists can keep track of everyone." Then he pointed to a man dressed all in black on a motorbike passing our bus. Motorbikes were everywhere and it seemed everybody owned one. They were the status-symbol transportation of this sorry society. You took your life in your hands crossing a street. I was even sideswiped by one of them in Saigon. The man in black was wearing a helmet with the shaded visor down. I had seen him or someone like him driving by before. They were the only ones wearing helmets.

"They've got earphones and microphones in those helmets," Michael said. "They're reporting back everything we do."

We convoyed out to the area where our Wheaton grad's helicopter was reported to have crashed, and started reconning

205

around. Of course, it was raining. We hiked the boonies one last time, wading through Elephant Grass again. It felt great—not the Elephant Grass, but the experience. Elephant Grass grows to some ten feet in length and derives its name from the fact that the elephants eat it. Their tongues must be as tough as their hides; the Elephant Grass is razor sharp. If you absent-mindedly let your hand run along it as you walk, its cuts you, bad enough that you never do it again.

We found fragments of a helicopter seat, but nothing much else. Then we pulled out our wallets and bribed the locals. That did the trick! Several came forth, selling us dog tags and even military I.D. cards they had kept for more than 25 years. An older man related how he saw the helicopter on fire blow up over a nearby field. He told us the engine sat out there in the field for decades, only to be hauled away for scrap two years ago.

We kept the tags and cards, but copied the information down in a small notebook just to be safe.

At dinner that night, one of the two government guides that went with us (I dubbed them Frick and Frack) began asking "friendly" questions:

"Your interpreter, he was born in Vietnam?" asked the beautiful young woman.

"Sure," someone answered. "Michael was one of the kids flown out in 1975 during the fall of Saigon. An American doctor and his family adopted him."

"And where does he live now in the United States?" she asked me.

"You'd better ask him," I replied. I turned back to my meal. There was something not quite right here. She was asking too many personal questions.

Later, as she walked away, one of the guys spotted a bulge in the back of her sweater. "Look, she's wired," he said.

Hoot in the Cu Chi Tunnels.

That night, Hoot pulled me aside. "Frick and Frack have Michael in a room alone interrogating him. Let's get him out of there."

Without knocking, we pushed open the door and walked in with all the American false bravado of a vintage Mitchum movie. We were both six-footers and 200 pounds, which didn't hurt. We were also well past our primes, which didn't help. Then we went into our act.

"Hey, Michael, what's keeping you? This looks like a boring party, Man," I said. "Let's blow this Popsicle stand."

The Vietnamese/American interpreter—who spoke both languages fluently, was always smiling, and who could joke in English with the best of us—looked at us like we were the U.S. Cavalry.

I was.

"He's an American now," Hoot told Frick and Frack as we left. "You don't have any hold on him anymore." We left the startled pair sitting on the bed.

That night, the Commies snuck into our rooms, stole the dog tags and I.D. cards we'd collected, and even tore out the single page of the notebook where their numbers were recorded—all without waking us. They knew everything we'd been doing. It was Orwell's *Animal Farm* and *1984* alive and well in Southeast Asia.

The Japanese and Germans lost World War II. Yet, at my house you'd never know it; you'd think they'd won. In my garage and driveway sit a Honda, a Subaru, and a 1998 BMW. Their cars—like their economics—are some of the best in the world.

Countries that lose to the United States inevitably end up better off than if they'd won. The Vietnamese should have gleaned that from history and thrown the war; lost it on purpose. If they had, we might have rebuilt their industry, too, and today I might be driving a "Minhmobile" . . . "I'll take the new 'Ho' with the revolutionary red metallic exterior, please."

I guess I'd never really admitted we lost the war in Vietnam, not deep down in my heart of hearts, until that return trip. It happened suddenly, in a most unlikely place.

We were at an outdoor café, eating lunch on the beach along the South China Sea. The ocean breeze was refreshing and the meal, like all the food we enjoyed during our eleven-day trip, was excellent. Then the sound of jets overhead captured our attention. There were four of them, streaking through the cloudless sky like something out of the Fourth of July—except they were Russian MiG-21s!

That's when I knew we had lost.

Returning to Vietnam in 1995, seeing how the Communists still treated people, was the only time in my life since the war that I actually regretted not carrying a weapon. But the regret didn't last, and if I had it to do all over again, I'd make the same decision.

It's been said that life is a gift. It's not. It's a loan. That's why the Lender reclaims it at the end. So we had better invest our loan wisely, because all we'll have in the end is the interest we've earned. That's our gift . . . to Him.

In Vietnam, I took a big risk and gambled my life's blood— and it paid off to the tune of some five lives, buying them years they would not have had otherwise. What it cost me personally pales in comparison to the satisfaction I still feel decades later.

I like to think the Lender was satisfied, too. I did it for Him.

Final Lesson: You *CAN* walk through the Valley of Death . . . you just have to follow in the right footsteps.

When I see someone wearing a Nam hat, fatigue jacket, or a unit tattoo, I'm always taken back by how old he looks. His hair is either all gray or all gone, he's paunchy, wears glasses, and maybe even has a hearing aid. If not exactly an old man, he's doing a pretty fair imitation.

That's what I like about the guys I served with in combat— they come in the same category as the girls I dated in high school—forever young. Memory is great in that regard, it's selective, like those old late-night movies where our favorite actors never age, never die.

Mirrors are mostly a matter of memory, too. When we look at ourselves, we see what we want to see, how we were rather than how we are. That's why photographs are such a shock to our systems. They are much less user-friendly. They capture a moment in time, an instant, rather than a memory—and they do so in the harshest of lighting, so that every line, every scar, and every blemish show.

I've never made a 1st Cav or 1/9th reunion. I don't need to see my guys again, not the way they are today, after life has beaten them down and dowsed the flames of their spirits. And I don't need to hear them missing at roll call. I'd rather remember them the way they were, the way I was.

To this day, whenever I hear a Vietnam-era Huey overhead with its signature "Whop! Whop! Whop!" I think of C Troop. I imagine it landing, with Marty, Bratch, and Weise all in one row, Matt on the radio, and Smitty behind the machine gun. Except this time the weapon is absent. Then I look to the left and see that my niche next to the engine firewall is empty.

"Come on, Doc!" Bratch yells above the howling storm of beating blades. "We ain't got all day. There's one more mission . . ."

The End

Post Script: Name Change

Most of those I served with in Vietnam were brave, good men. They would have been heroes in anybody's book, in anybody's war, throughout our history. What I've told about them is true from my recollections and what I recorded in my letters home, written at the time. Some names I've changed for obvious reasons—like those who died badly. Some I've changed for not so obvious reasons—like the handful who lived badly. Mostly, however, I've changed names for my own personal reasons, including not causing any more pain to some who have suffered too much already.

John "Marty" Martin, Charles Roberts, Jim "Weece" Weise, Bratch, Bethel "Smitty" Smith, Ken Williams, Jorge Martinez, Jerry Ware, Bob "Hoot" Hooten, Gary Barfoot, Bill Vanover, Doc Row, Doc Shore, Doc Barkley, WO John Hazelwood, Sgt. Henley, Sgt. Kaneshiro, Sgt. Haskett, Sgt. Samuel, and Sgt. Cain are the real names of my real vet friends I haven't changed. Matt—Matthew Brennan—our FO is a noted author himself. In fact, he went to war for the expressed purpose of writing about the experience. His magnificent memoir, *Flashing Saber,* and his riveting autobiography of life after Vietnam, *Broken Helmet,* are must reads.

Whether we were a "Band of Brothers" or more like a "Gang of Cousins," we were—and always will be—family. Blood is thicker than water, and blood spilled for one another is the thickest of all. Even the jungle cannot soak it up.

Etched on the Black Wall are the names of 1,354 Medics who gave their all in the Vietnam War; 184 of them from the 1st Air Cav Division. This is my tribute to them—the book they didn't live to write. Its pages are my piece of the war . . . and that's the only peace most of us will ever have from any war.

About the Author

Brad L. Smith has a Master of Arts degree with honor in Journalism from Wheaton College Graduate School and more than 40 years of experience as a professional writer. He has been a journalist/photographer in Sudan, Uganda, Venezuela, Ecuador, Southern Mexico, and Vietnam (1995). BLSmith is also the playwright of *The Man from Aldersgate,* which has been performed some 2,000 times in all 50 states and 32 countries since 1979. This one-man play starring Roger Nelson (and now B.J. Johnston, following Mr. Nelson's retirement in 2017) also became the Silver Angel Award's Best New Video for 1989.

Brad lives with his wife, Donna, in California. She is a teacher. The couple's married daughter, Christine, is a Nurse Practitioner.

Look for other Amazon paperbacks and Kindle eBook by this author, including *Track of the Panzer*, his World War II novel; and *Bought and Soldier*, the Civil War-leg of Smith's war trilogy.

Brad's latest book is *Epitaph in Red Leather*, a hard-hitting sport's novel.

Photo by Eric Negron

About the Photographs

All captioned photographs were taken by the author (or of him) in Vietnam in 1967 and 1995 and are his sole property, apart from those by Matthew Brennan, Sgt. Tong, and Eric Negron. The remaining, non-captioned photos are Public Domain.

Made in the USA
Middletown, DE
16 October 2017